On the Shoulders

of *Just*[1] Folks

Faye Robinson Owens

---

[1] *Just*: (1) guided by truth, reason, justice, and fairness; (7) (especially in Biblical use) righteous; (12) only or merely (dictionary.com).

ISBN 978-1-63961-651-0 (paperback)
ISBN 978-1-63961-652-7 (digital)

Christian Faith Publishing
832 Park Avenue
Meadville, PA 16335
www.christianfaithpublishing.com

Printed in the United States of America

Dedication

With love and gratitude, I dedicate *On the Shoulders of Just Folks* to my loving husband, confidant, and best friend, Douglas Owens, who has been my companion since childhood. Together, Doug and I have celebrated many of these stories. Together, by God's grace, we have overcome the others.

The angels are the dispensers and administrators of the divine benefi-
cence toward us; they regard our safety, undertake our defense, direct
our ways, and exercise a constant solicitude that no evil befall us.

—John Calvin, *Institutes of the Christian Religion*

Our family story, as it was told to me and as I experienced it,
is written as a legacy to my children:
Debra Lynn (Owens) Bennett and my son-in-law Greg Bennett,
Sharilyn Kay Owens and my son-in-law Randy Gambill;
and to my grandchildren:
Thomas, James Douglas (JD), Elizabeth, and Noah.

Acknowledgments

I express sincere thanks to my family and friends who, along my publishing journey, read the manuscript and contributed feedback from their respective banks of expertise, memories, editing skills, and commendations in support of *Just* Folks:

- Mary Nell Roos, my dear friend who has pushed me to write the book since hearing my half-told story forty years ago;
- Rev. Albert Kennington is not only my hometown friend and high school classmate. He was organist at my wedding and my contender for teacher's pet in English class. Albert is a former English teacher, a retired Episcopal priest, and a published author;
- Dr. Rob Blackaby, president of Canadian Baptist Theological Seminary and College in Cochrane, Alberta, who, along with his faculty, staff, and extended family, continue their mission to train men and women to share the gospel throughout Canada and beyond;
- Rev. Phil Waldrep, evangelist and author, who is the founder and CEO of Phil Waldrep Ministries based in Decatur, Alabama. Phil and his ministry team annually organize Women of Joy, Gridiron Men's Conference, Celebrators Conference, and Pastors' Encouragement Retreat. Doug and I have been blessed by attending thirteen of Phil's last fourteen Celebrators Conferences in Sevierville and Pigeon Forge, Tennessee;

- Hope Taft, who is my friend, my former neighbor, a master gardener, and Ohio's first lady (1999–2007). Hope is the president of the board for the Tandana Foundation, which focuses on health care, gardening, and community structure to empower communities in Ecuador, Mali, and West Africa;
- Levi Kirkland, my ninety-year-old maternal uncle who has always been my rock, even begging my mother not to give me, a toddler, a daily dose of cod liver oil;
- Last but not least, Greg, Debra, Sharilyn, and others in my dear family who read and respectfully gave their candid suggestions. And there's always my dear Doug…always.

Prologue

Anna shook off the chill of the early October morning. Standing just outside her front door, she could hear Viola's groans as her daughter-in-law's labor pains were becoming more frequent and more intense. Dismissing her thoughts to return inside to grab a shawl, Anna refocused on the urgency of her mission, clutched her arms across her chest, and squeezed them tightly to provide a little warmth as she walked briskly head-on into the north wind to summon the help of a neighbor.

Tom and Lula Jones were prominent farmers in the Martinville community just north of the bustling little farm town of Atmore, Alabama, on the Florida state line. The smell of bacon frying was a welcomed relief, assuring Anna that Lula was home. Pounding emphatically on the front door, Anna was greeted by Lula drying her hands on her apron and inviting her out-of-breath neighbor inside. Distracted and somewhat alarmed by his neighbor's early-hour arrival, Tom quickly threw the last bale of hay to his dairy cows and rushed in from the barn to find Lula and Anna warming in front of the wood-burning cookstove. Anna graciously declined the offer of coffee, although the aroma was tempting as the beverage perked in the blue-speckled enamel pot.

"Viola is in labor," Lula informed Tom. "Can you drive her to the hospital?"

Tom grabbed the keys to his pickup truck and, with a whistle, summoned his sidekick Smokey, a German police dog, who was as vicious as he was beautiful, to take his guard position in the bed of the pickup. With help now assured, Anna calmly climbed into the truck's passenger seat. Driving the half mile to the Robinson's attractive bungalow home with its vine-covered, white latticework front-porch privacy screen, Tom broke the silence, "Anna, I thought Lula said that baby was due in November. Is everything okay?"

"I hope so," Anna replied. "Viola said she tripped over Herman's dog, Monie, this morning, and the labor pains started. I pray everything is going to be all right."

Herman was the youngest of the four sons of Anna and Zollie Robinson. He joined the Navy in June 1943 following his eighteenth birthday in March. Aubrey, the Robinson's second oldest, was married to Eunice and enlisted in the Army. Thomas Marshall (named for the vice president in the administration [1913–1921] of President Woodrow Wilson), son number 3 and the father of Viola's baby, was in Virginia awaiting World War II overseas deployment with the Army Air Force. Vernon was the oldest son. Vernon's heart murmur, probably caused by Anna's serious bout with rheumatic fever during her pregnancy, prevented Vernon from qualifying for military service. Four years earlier, Vernon and Margaret had given Zollie and Anna their first grandchild, Gloria Ann.

Smokey offered a paltry growl as Tom gingerly assisted pregnant Viola into the passenger seat of the truck. There was no room for an additional passenger in the pickup, so Anna retreated into her house to pray and wait until someone could personally deliver the news. Party-line phone service was not available to residents of Martinville until more than a decade later.

Meanwhile, at Vaught Hospital in Atmore, a baby girl arrived at 4:25 p.m. Viola, age twenty-one, had endured labor and delivered her baby, with the help of Dr. Alfred J. Treherne, with no husband nor family member to comfort her in her pain nor to celebrate with her after delivery. Squeezing her pink bundle with the pride, love, and joy that only a new mother can know, Viola called to the registrar, who was nearby, documenting the delivery for the birth certificate. "Look! She has dimples! I have always heard that a baby has dimples when she or he has been kissed by an angel."

Mrs. Woodson, the registrar, nodded and offered a courtesy smile as she dutifully focused on her government-required recording of the birth data. As Viola proofread the document for accuracy, she privately struggled with the realization that "full-term pregnancy" now recorded on a permanent record would reveal the secret that she and Marshall had kept for eight months and that the made-up story of her premature labor caused by tripping over the pet dog was a cover-up. Continuing to provide information to the registrar, Viola emphasized, "I promised my five-year-old youngest sister, Glenda Joyce, that the baby would have her name. Her middle name will be Faye as a namesake for my best friend, Faye Coon, the sweetest and most trustworthy person I have ever known. My baby's name is Joyce Faye."

My Tribute

I am that "kissed by the angels" baby. Now in my late seventies and looking back over my lifetime, I am compelled to tell the story of my life's amazing journey: my tribute to common folks who were strategically and timely placed to alter and/or to encourage my life's next chapter.

In the 1940s and 1950s, sightings of giants in south Alabama were extremely rare, depending on the storyteller's spin. As a child, I saw no one with colossal size akin to the biblical character Goliath, nor the mythical "fee fie fo fum" ogre depicted in *Jack and the Beanstalk*. Well, maybe a few were close. Those I have encountered throughout my life are ordinary people whose virtues of selflessness and commitment to the well-being of others far surpassed what may have seemed lacking in their Zacchaeus-size statures. Having no shoulders of iconic giants on which to stand, my spiritual, emotional, physical, and professional development from conception has been secured while on the shoulders and in the altruistic hearts of *just* folks. Their investment in my welfare averted what could have been a chaotic childhood and assured my becoming a secure adult with goals, dreams, determination, gratitude, and fond memories. I write my grateful story in tribute to these dear people, my surrogate giants in south Alabama, Georgia, Canada, Ohio, and beyond, many of whom never knew of the impact he or she contributed.

Soldier, Husband, and Father—AWOL (Absent without *Letters*)

Mother proudly bonded with her new baby. The two of us were inseparable. Life had not been easy for her since Dad's enlistment in April 1942. They had a hastily arranged marriage after learning of Mother's pregnancy. A war bride, now with a baby in tow, Mother continued living intermittently for the next three years with her parents, her sister and brother-in-law, and her parents-in-law. It was humiliating for her to solely rely on the charity of others, but Mother was unemployed and needed housing, food, and help to care for her new baby. She managed the awkwardness of home-hopping: when she wore out her welcome with one family, she moved on.

Mother with baby Faye

The care and fostering provided by my paternal grandparents during my first three impressionable years were providential.

Mother shared some sobering stories with me when I was probably forty-something. At the time of my birth, there were two other babies born within the same week in small-town Atmore's hospital. Two of the newborns were to wives of soldiers who were still stateside in training at the same military base in Virginia and awaiting deployment. The soldiers were given short-term passes to return home to see their wives and babies. According to Mother, my dad declined the temporary leave. I have maintained a "kinship" with the other two babies: my classmates and lifelong friends, Mary Helen and Leonard, whom I first met in the maternity ward nursery at Atmore Vaught Hospital.

When Mother's lodging rotation brought her to Atmore to stay with her parents-in-law, she daily watched for the rural mail delivery truck, hoping to hear from her husband. Dad, an Army airplane mechanic, was now serving in fierce World War II combat in northern Italy and France. Letters were few and, according to Mother, when the occasional correspondence arrived, the mail was addressed to his parents with no mention of her nor his child. She felt even more deeply the pain of isolation and rejection. The most disturbing, and indeed the most emotionally painful story, was that before Dad's departure from Atmore, he apparently gave Mother a slip of paper on which was written the name of his local pharmacist friend who could advise her about and assist her with an abortion.

In 1944, Mother and I traveled by train, a common mode of wartime transportation, to Santa Fe where Dad's brother, Aubrey, and sister-in-law, Eunice, were expecting their first child. Mother went with the intent to help Aunt Eunice with her baby due in October. Instead, Mother got a much-needed job working in the Army commissary where Uncle Aubrey was manager. Apparently, it was decided that income from Mother's employment would be more beneficial to help pay living expenses. It was an interesting turn of events that Mother went to help Aunt Eunice, but Aunt Eunice not only took care of her newborn, Wayne, but she also looked after me.

3

Mother and Aunt Eunice nurtured a strong friendship that endured the brewing storms of Mother's divorce yet to come.

Aunt Eunice told two stories about me while under her watch in New Mexico. She had left me alone with baby Wayne while she quickly hung diapers on the backyard clothesline. When she returned, I was trying to help Wayne stop crying by holding a pillow over his face. Thankfully, she came back before any harm was inflicted on my infant cousin, who soon became one of my best buddies, and we continued that affection until his death from cancer in 2012. Another shared story from Aunt Eunice was that while in her care, I, a lively two-year-old, fell face-first onto the hot pot-bellied stove and suffered a severe burn on my cheek. She feared my face would be scarred for life, but the burn soon healed with no lasting effects. It was in Santa Fe when, at age two, I duly and lovingly acquired the nickname Droopy Drawers that Uncle Aubrey called me, in private or in public, until his death in 1999.

A large professionally framed picture of my dad in uniform hung in the long entrance hall of my Robinson grandparents' home.

My Sweet Daddy

4

That image of my handsome dad was first introduced to me when I was a babe in arms. My Robinson family thought it was cute that I had been taught to respond on cue to "Who is that?" with "That is my sweet daddy," resulting in laughter and hugs for me from visiting family and friends.

Mammaw treasured that picture. Ironically, when I was a teenager, she would sometimes scowl as she referenced Mother's lavish spending on expensive family pictures and motion toward that picture of "my sweet daddy." On the contrary, I have treasured those pictures, including some professionally produced baby portraits of me. They fill a void in my memory that I otherwise would not have.

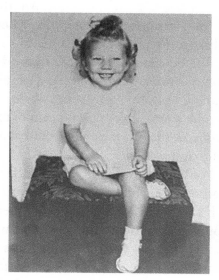

Three-year-old Faye

Daddy returned home from World War II overseas service the day before my third birthday. The taxi arrived at the front gate of his parents' home. Mother awakened me from my bed located beside a window that gave a clear view of my dad's arrival, a celebration forever etched in my memory. Mother told me that she quickly wiped the sleepiness from my face, ran a brush through my blonde Shirley Temple curls, and ushered me to the front porch. Mother tried to encourage me, apparently still in a sleepy fog, to overcome my hesitation to rush to Daddy waiting at the front gate. She prompted me several times by asking, "Do you know who that is?" She reported that finally I sassily put my hand on my hip, flipped my hair, looked back at her as I ran down the steps and into his arms, and responded, "Yes, I know who it is. He is my sweet daddy."

The next day's reunion of Daddy's safe return home was combined with the celebration of my third birthday.

The joyful celebration was short-lived. My parents, who were now reunited after three and a half years, moved into a room above Dad's brother, Uncle Vernon's, gas station in Jackson, Alabama. Uncle Vernon gave Daddy a job at the station. Aunt Margaret prepared short-order meals for sale to their customers. An irrelevant memory, but traumatic for me, was once I was hopping from one five-gallon lard can to another in the café's pantry. One of the lids was loose. When I jumped, the lid came off, and I fell into the lard up to my shoulders. In that era, prior to Proctor and Gamble's Dawn detergent, much scrubbing in warm soapy water was necessary to get the grease off me. No one was angry or upset. I cannot report on whether the grease remaining in the can was reused for baking or frying, but I'm willing to bet that it was.

My doctor's office was in his house in Jackson, and it had a beautiful white arbor gate with trellis roses. That is my only pleasant memory of his practice because my visits there were typically for whooping cough vaccinations and other pediatric care. Mother and Daddy accompanied me, age three, to a Jackson dentist where a simple toothache almost cost my life. While dental associates were prepping me to evaluate the integrity of the tooth, Mother observed through a slightly opened door from the waiting room that the attendants were frantically scurrying about in the room where I was being treated. Mother's instincts alerted her to rush through the closed door where I was unresponsive from an apparent overdose of the medication given to sedate me. Daddy rushed in and using some maneuver/technique, he was able to revive me. Until Mother's death, seventy years later, she always cautioned any time that I was scheduled for a medical procedure that gas could be lethal for me.

Divorce and Custody Battle

Daddy and Mother were together only a few weeks when rumors of Mother's infidelity began to surface. Instead of retreating to their anticipated delayed honeymoon, storm clouds began to gather, and divorce proceedings became imminent. Although I was barely three, some of my first memories were sensing tension and uneasiness as the three of us walked beside a creek. I remember seeing Daddy skipping small pebbles across the water's surface. I also remember being hoisted onto his shoulders to get a good look into a split-rail fence pigpen that corralled hogs, piglets, and the raunchy smell of slop. It was perhaps on that same outing that I was riding in the back seat of the car and playing with my doll. My curiosity piqued when I overheard Mother warn Daddy of my presence and say to him, "Stop! I don't want Faye to hear that!" Of course, I remember that at this caution that I should not be hearing *something*, I leaned forward to try to catch every word that was not meant for my tender ears!

When Dad confirmed the heartbreaking truth of an affair, their four-year marriage, most of which was interrupted by Dad's military service, ended in divorce. On July 12, 1946, my dad, Marshall Robinson, filed in the Circuit Court, Clarke County, Alabama, his bill of complaint versus my mother, Viola Robinson, respondent. The reason set forth in the legal document stated that "prior to the seventh day of July 1946, respondent committed acts of adultery."

Three days later, on July 10, 1946, Mother, respondent, filed an Answer and Waiver to the Circuit Court, Grove Hill, Alabama: "Viola Robinson, the person named as defendant in this cause and

7

for answer to the bill, herein says she denies each and every allegation therein and demands strict proof of the same."

The "strict proof" that Mother had requested was met with a deposition taken on oral examination on July 12, 1946, in the presence of Q. W. Tucker, registrar, and Paul S. Jones, the attorney for my dad, the complainant. In addition to Dad's testimony, Vernon and Margaret Robinson, Daddy's brother and sister-in-law, gave depositions as material witnesses. America had rallied around her returning war heroes. The consensus would likely be, how dare a spouse be unfaithful while the troops were risking all for their country? I think this patriotism tipped the decision in Dad's favor when on July 15, 1946, he was awarded "permanent custody and control" of his child, whom he had met only a few months earlier. Apparently, in addition to the "documented" account of adultery presented to the court, there were rumors that Mother had another affair during Dad's deployment. With suspicions of her misconduct, Mother was apparently reprimanded by her parents, who were caring for me, a baby, during the day while Mother worked at a temporary job when the alleged affair took place.

Mother's perceived adulterous reputation and the court documents defined her as an unfit mother. Unfit as a wife, apparently yes; but as a mother, definitely not. Mother adored me and, above everything else, she lovingly and sacrificially cared about my well-being. She would always use a memorable parenting skill to gently talk through disciplinary issues with me. If I denied instigating or participating in any wrongdoing, she would admonish me to tell her the truth. Mother would say, "If you did it, tell me the truth, and you will not be in trouble. But if you tell me a story [lie] and I find out you did not tell the truth, then you will be in trouble." That concept worked well for all our lives, even when I had to become the parent and she the child.

During my first three years with her, Mother gave me a daily dose of cod liver oil. It was so routine that I didn't even complain. On the other hand, Mother's brother, Levi, eleven years older than I, would plead with his sister to please not give me that "disgusting stuff!" That disgusting stuff has apparently played a significant role in my excellent health for three quarters of a century.

While cleaning out my stepmother's house following her death in 2014, I found among my previously deceased dad's belongings a handwritten letter postmarked in my maternal grandparents' hometown, Castleberry, Alabama, June 26, 1946, a couple of weeks before the divorce proceedings. Grandmother Kirkland had written the personal letter to her daughter, Wilma (Mother's sister), and son-in-law, Bill, lovingly addressing Mother's fragile health following an appendectomy, inquiring about my welfare, and expressing Grandmother's prayer that Mother and Daddy would not divorce. Grandmother wrote that she felt sorry for my dad, did not blame him, supported his decision to get a divorce, hoped Mother would change for the better, and expressed hope for reconciliation. Unless Aunt Wilma gave that letter to my dad to help his custody case against her sister, there was no other way Dad could have come into possession of it.

Mother disclosed the following story to me when I was an adult. Before the judge ruled the custody decision in Dad's favor, but they were not living together, Daddy drove Mother and me to the small community of Pollard, Alabama, where Uncle Alvin and Aunt Doris (Mother's sister) lived with their two young daughters. With no phones to communicate on short notice, Alvin and Doris did not know that Mother and I were coming. An additional sign of the times was that, although they were not home, the doors to their run-down house were unlocked. According to Mother, when Daddy pushed her from the car with me in her arms, she turned and said to him, "I have no money and no food."

He responded, "Tough beans," as he drove away. Walking into the unlocked house and finding no one home, Mother searched their kitchen for food. Finding none, and while I was crying, Mother began to panic. Other than her sister's family, Mother did not know any people in Pollard, and she didn't know how long Alvin and Doris would be gone. Darkness was falling when the two of us walked the deserted lone street through town. By this time, Mother was crying too. She got the attention of a woman who was working alone in her yard. When Mother explained our plight, the dear angel entered her house and returned to press five one-dollar bills into Mother's hand. Quickly making our way to the one small general store in Pollard, Mother purchased enough food to feed us for a couple of days. Five bucks was a lot of money in 1946. When we returned to Alvin and Doris's house, they were home. Mother told them our story. Uncle Alvin searched his house, came up with five dollars in bills and coins, and dashed off that late evening to repay the benevolent neighbor. From what I observed five years later as a child, when spending a summer with my Kirkland family, my aunt and uncle lived from hand to mouth in their poverty. They later divorced when struggling Uncle Alvin could no longer control his addiction to alcohol.

The difficult day came for Mother to move from the upstairs gas-station apartment that she had shared with Dad and me. Somewhat oblivious to the seriousness of the moment, I watched with Uncle Alvin, Mother's then brother-in-law, who had come with her in his truck to move her belongings. Mother and Uncle Alvin stood on the ground while Daddy literally threw her clothes and other possessions from the upstairs deck to Uncle Alvin on the ground below. From that day forward, those two men had it in for each other.

Some years later, Daddy was married to Beryl and living in our hometown of Atmore, Alabama. The Alaflora Fair was an exciting fall carnival, livestock exhibition, midway, and fireworks show. The event was big-time entertainment drawing large crowds from southwest Alabama and northwest Florida. I overheard family members discussing that Marshall (my dad) had learned that Uncle Alvin was coming that night to the fair. Apparently, he and Uncle Alvin had fisticuffs later that evening after meeting at a predetermined place near the fairgrounds. Dad found amusement in later sharing that in route to the fracas, he had stopped by the Atmore police station to ask the amount of the fine for assault and battery. Upon learning the monetary penalty, he laid the cash on the officer's desk and proceeded to the confrontation.

Tranquil Transitions

Before his marriage to Beryl in 1949 and while a single parent living in Jackson, Dad tried to provide for me while the now two of us lived above the gas station, and he continued working with and for his brother. My cousin, Gloria, Uncle Vernon and Aunt Margaret's daughter, walked with me to the two-week half-day sessions of Vacation Bible School (VBS) at First Baptist Church (FBC), Jackson. Gloria, age seven, responsibly accompanied me, age three, to my classroom door each morning. Gloria met me at that designated place to walk me home after VBS was dismissed. "Home" was the apartment above her dad's gas station. Bro. Ketchum was the compassionate pastor at FBC, Jackson, who always squatted to the child's level as he daily welcomed each one. I looked forward to his greeting. It's amazing how that small, kind gesture left a lasting positive impression.

As for any single parent, managing a job and providing suitable care for a child had its share of hardships and scheduling conflicts for Daddy. I am uncertain if the original arrangements were temporary or long-term, but another turn of fate was when I found myself back in Atmore in the care of my paternal grandparents. Those earlier days of moving with Mother from relative to relative had apparently trained my young emotions to be trusting and resilient. To help their son as he transitioned to civilian life as a single father, my grandparents, at ages fifty-seven and fifty-eight, welcomed the opportunity to raise me as the daughter they had always wanted. Because I had already experienced my grandparents' love and care for me and for Mother, their now ex-daughter-in-law, I was emotionally secure in one of my happy places, and I do not remember any separation anxiety whatsoever. I don't remember ever asking for or crying for my mother nor for my daddy, but I seamlessly adjusted to life with my nurturing grandparents. *Neither my grandparents nor I realized that this was the pivotal first day of the rest of my life.*

Pawpaw and his grands: Gloria, baby Wayne, and Faye

My grandparents, lovingly called Pawpaw and Mammaw by their eight grandchildren, lived in a two-bedroom white bungalow that they had built in 1938. The white lattice wisteria-covered trellis shaded the front porch and welcomed neighbors and family to come sit, rock, or swing as shared stories, laughter, and sometimes songs abounded. At harvest time, any drop-in visitors were likely to be handed a pan to join in the shelling of peas or beans.

The house had a guest room with one double bed. Mammaw and Pawpaw's bedroom had two double beds. All beds boasted handmade feather mattresses. At age three, when I arrived as their little girl, Pawpaw moved from sharing the bed with his wife of thirty-six years to the adjacent empty bed. I took his place at Mammaw's side.

During the night, if I squirmed or became restless, I would feel Mammaw's hand gently patting or rubbing my arm or leg and whispering, "It's okay, honey. It's okay." When worry now occasionally invades my mind to cause the adult-me to toss and turn and robs me of sleep, I am reassured when I remember Mammaw's encouraging words, "It's okay, honey. It's okay."

Uncle Herman, in his early twenties, was discharged from the U.S. Navy at the end of World War II after serving in the Pacific theater on the USS *Arctic* and the USS *Feland*. He returned home and lived with his parents and me for a short time until he enrolled at the University of Southern Mississippi to pursue a degree in education. Although I was quite young, I was concerned that after he seemed to enjoy his mother's home-cooked meals, Uncle Herman would often quickly leave the table and run outside to vomit. Today's medical diagnostics would have likely confirmed his condition as post-traumatic stress disorder (PTSD).

When Mammaw, Pawpaw, and I returned home from Robinsonville Baptist Church's 1947 Christmas Eve program, Pawpaw entered our house first. He walked to the dining room table and yanked the pull chain. Not only did the ceiling light come on, but the turntable on a child's 78 rpm record player began to spin and play. I was so surprised that Santa (aka Uncle Herman) had already come and delivered my requested record player.

Soon after moving to live with my grandparents, they upgraded from fireplaces to gas space heaters. Some winter nights, even in south Alabama, temperatures would drop to freezing or below. Space heaters, though an improvement over fireplaces, did not provide the efficient, consistent warmth of today's controlled central heating. At bedtime on wintry nights, Mammaw would regularly warm a large bath towel in front of the heater. Then she would then roll me up like an enchilada and tuck me between the cold bedsheets.

Recurring thoughts of afternoon naps bring pleasant memories. Mammaw's cooking the midday meal (that we called dinner because it was the big meal of the day) from scratch on and in a wood-burning stove in Alabama's summer heat with no air conditioning was exhausting. Plus, now having the unexpected responsibilities of

13

caring for an active three-year-old, Mammaw welcomed afternoon nap time. I would lie beside Mammaw on top of her bed covers. The opened screened windows not only provided a welcomed slight stirring of air created by the fanned breezes of giant oaks, but also brought the intoxicatingly sweet fragrances of mimosas, gardenias, and wisterias. The cackle of the hens, pot-racking of the guineas, and the occasional clanging of Nellie's cowbell crooned a sweet and effective lullaby.

I sometimes gazed, mystified, at the light fixture in the middle of the bedroom ceiling. Inside the outlet was a screw-in gadget combining a double outlet with a light bulb socket having a pull-chain or string attached. Another outlet component of the contraption transitioned, as needed, from plugging in the oscillating fan to plugging in the iron. There were no wall outlets. It was underneath this multipurpose fixture, with an electric cord dangling from the ceiling socket outlet to her iron, that Mammaw spent hours ironing Pawpaw's hand-washed and stiffly starched shirts and, except for towels, socks, and underwear, all of our freshly laundered clothing.

Before getting her wringer-type Maytag washer shortly after my moving in, Mammaw hand-washed clothes outdoors using a wooden paddle to stir dirty laundry in a large cast-iron washpot. Another must-have on washday was a scrubboard to clean the dingiest farm clothes by rubbing the overalls on the ridged surface. Scrubboards are still available, mostly repurposed as a bluegrass musical instrument. I vaguely remember that when I was a toddler, homemade lye soap was a staple for washing floors and clothes. Like quilting parties where women sewed and socialized, women from the community would gather to cook and share the large batches of soap made from a recipe using leftover cooking fats and lye collected from leached hardwood ashes. The lye soap product was too harsh for bathing. Even when used for laundry, clothes were rinsed in two separate large galvanized washtubs to remove any residue before hanging the laundry to dry outdoors by pinning with clothespins on a long wire or rope clothesline suspended between two posts or trees. Weather predictions were unreliable at best. A summer pop-up shower summoned all hands to quickly gather the clothes inside to finish drying by hanging over chairs or another makeshift dryer.

Sometime later, perhaps a year, there was a devastating fire that destroyed Uncle Vernon's gas station, including Daddy's upstairs living quarters. I was around five years old at the time when all the Jackson-based family, including Daddy, returned to the Atmore area; however, I heard the gas-station fire story for the first time in 2019. All the adults who experienced the disaster are now deceased, so details are sketchy. Uncle Vernon and Aunt Margaret apparently lost everything. Thankfully, there were no injuries nor fatalities.

Following the disaster, Uncle Vernon temporarily relocated his family from Jackson to Bay Minette, Alabama, to readjust and contemplate what would be next. I vaguely remember sitting on the floor of an almost empty room. Gloria and I played on the floor while Mammaw, Pawpaw, Aunt Margaret, and Uncle Vernon sat in chairs in a somber discussion. My clearer and happier memories consist of frequent visits to Uncle Vernon and family's subsequent rental homes in Atmore and after Pawpaw's death, to their own home adjacent to Mammaw's house in the Martinville community.

Relocated in his hometown of Atmore, Daddy was rehired by his prewar employer, G. R. Swift, to his job with Swift Hunter Lumber Company. Daddy moved in with his parents and me in rural Atmore. A small room was added for him by enclosing the north end of a screened back porch that ran the entire east length of the house. His room was furnished with a single bed for sleeping, a chair, a small table, and a popular furniture piece for that era. Chifforobes were first advertised in the 1908 Sears, Roebuck & Company catalogue, which described the furniture as "a modern invention." Its design had three or four drawers stacked to about halfway the six-foot height. A shelf, used as a dressing table with a mirror, conveniently sat atop the drawer space. The parallel side had a mirrored door opening to a small clothes closet. Occasionally, Daddy would pull a picture from one of the drawers. He would ask me if I knew the man in military uniform who was kneeling on the sidewalk and talking to me. I did not know the man, but I am now convinced that Daddy was suspicious that the handsome soldier was one of Mother's suitors.

Cousins as Siblings

My close bond with cousins Gloria and Wayne solidly developed in our early years. Their parents invited me to participate in many of their family outings, including playtime at either of their respective homes or at Mammaw and Pawpaw's house and even overnight trips with Uncle Aubrey's family to visit Aunt Eunice's out-of-town parents or siblings. Mr. Brantley, Aunt Eunice's father, raised goats. His warped sense of humor included putting Wayne and me, usually just me (either because I was older or not his grandchild), into his goat pen. Mr. Brantley delighted in watching the goats harmlessly, but scary nonetheless, gently butt us kids (pun intended) around the pen.

I often wonder how Wayne and I survived some of our childhood shenanigans. On a particular day, the early morning rain had given way to partial sun, leaving lots of puddles to play in. I eagerly awaited Wayne's arrival. I wanted to share with him a newly discovered thrill. Our grandparents kept baby chicks in a brooder warmed by a light bulb until the cute little fluff-ball biddies developed into feathered adolescents. The pullets were then released among the other fowl in the chicken yard, and the young roosters were confined and fed in a coop awaiting butcher time. The last brood had been recently relocated and the light bulb removed. I have no idea what initially impressed me to insert my tiny finger into the empty electric socket, but it was that bone-tickling buzz that I wanted to share with Wayne. Mammaw, forever on the alert, along with our guardian angels working overtime when she had the two of us together, ran down the back porch steps, yelling, "No! No! No!"

Mammaw switched my legs on two occasions. Monitoring what Wayne and I might be up to, Mammaw looked out her kitchen window to the astonishing parade of numerous farm fowl chasing through the chicken yard with eggshells in their beaks. Coming to investigate, she found Wayne and me making mud pies in our pretend playhouse kitchen. Yes, literally *mud pies*. The main ingredients were dirt, water, and for this one time, eggs. Lots of eggs! The free-range eggs, along with milk, buttermilk, and butter, were a significant source of our extra income from neighbors who regularly purchased dairy products from our family. (Editorial note: At that time, we had not learned the term *free-range* for grading eggs because everyone's chickens were free-range on the farms. Pasteurized milk was available, but most folks in our town drank fresh raw milk because that is what we had.) As far as the trouble that Wayne and I were in, I told Mammaw that putting eggs in our mud pies was my idea, so please don't switch Wayne. She believed me, and I got the punishment. Wayne and I never lived down having our family tease us for using all Mammaw's hen eggs in our mud pie bake-off. On that occasion, if there were any bake-off "winners," it was Wayne.

The second spanking occurred when Mammaw and I were visiting Ms. Ima, our neighbor. I was about four years old and suffering from a common childhood eye infection. Ms. Ima offered her eye drops to soothe my discomfort. No one explained to me what the procedure would be. When Ms. Ima forcibly held me down for Mammaw to administer the drops, I bit Ms. Ima's arm. That was not a good strategy on my part. The eye drops were not the only application Mammaw administered on that day.

Gloria was four years older than I. Her sister, Sandra, was four years younger than I. Even with the age span, we cousins had so much fun together. We entertained ourselves and the household by listening to the 1950s rock and roll 45 rpm records. The one of us who was the movie star, vocalist, or comedian, would stand on a chair, peering through the glass window at the top half of the dining-room door. It was the perfect frame for our pretend TV screen. The other two girls, plus any adult passing through the room, played the part of the studio audience. The audience would laugh on cue, applaud, or sing along, entertained by our amazing imagination and talent. Often Tony, the parakeet, would squawk his opinion, "Tony is a party doll," mimicking the 1957 lyrics of the rock and roll legend, Buddy Knox. We designed ritzy homes using facecloths for bedding and created fashions for our paper dolls, sometimes purchased, but most often cut from expired Sears & Roebuck catalogs. Always young at heart, Gloria never outgrew her participation in our childhood pastimes. When her boyfriend, Merton Middleton, whom she married in 1959, arrived to pick her up for a date, Gloria would scramble to throw her paper dolls out of his view!

Sometimes our only two male cousins, Wayne and Don, were added to the mix. The five of us, home alone and ranging in age from Donald (six) to Gloria (sixteen), decided on a whim one morning to surprise Aunt Margaret with her favorite angel food cake when she came home for lunch from Vanity Fair Mills, a manufacturer of lingerie and a major employer of particularly Atmore-area women. Of course, not one of us had a clue, but upon finding a recipe, we were pleased that all ingredients were available, including a dozen eggs for beaten egg whites. All seemed under control until we realized that baking at 375 degrees, the cake would not be ready for Aunt Margaret's lunch break. What harm could come by increasing the temperature only 25 degrees to 400 degrees? When Aunt Margaret opened the door to announce her arrival, the smoked-filled kitchen had the stench of scorched cake. Aunt Margaret graciously bragged on our efforts as she tried to enjoy her dessert, made with love, although burnt on top and raw in the center.

My relationship with younger cousins, Sandra and Donald, became more meaningful when they became teenagers and especially now that the three of us are senior adults. The childhood age gap between us dissipated as we matured, and the friendship bond strengthened. Wayne, of course, had always been my buddy and partner in mischief. Gloria married Merton Middleton in January 1959, one month prior to Pawpaw's death. The newlyweds moved to Mobile, an hour's drive away.

On rare weekends, when Doug, my boyfriend (now husband), did not come home from Troy State College, Sandra, age fourteen, and I, four years older, would take a Sunday afternoon drive in my Ford Fairlane 500 to Monroeville, Alabama, or to Pensacola or Jay, Florida. Those were great times. In our safe environment, parents generally had no concerns about letting their children, especially teenagers, spread their wings and venture into adulthood. We would give our in-charge adults a probable destination, but if we changed our minds, we just went somewhere different. There were no cell phones to contact anyone if our plans changed. Thankfully, we always returned safely and in time for Sunday evening programs at church.

Mother's Attempts to Abduct Me

Mother never emotionally accepted the devastating finality of the court's custody decision. Losing access to her only child was unbearable. She set about scheming to get me back. On Mother's first attempt, she arrived in tears at the front door of my paternal grandparents' home, pleading with Mammaw, who was alone with me, age three, that morning. Mammaw was a sensitive and trusting lady whose tender heart was touched by Mother's story that my maternal grandmother had become quite ill. Mother begged that she be allowed to take me to visit her mother, and she promised to deliver me back on a given day. Dad lived and worked at his brother's gas station in Jackson, Alabama, a couple of hours' drive away, and Pawpaw worked at Atmore Prison Farm. Having no phone to get advice or approval, Mammaw packed my clothes and reluctantly watched as Mother carried me away in her arms to a waiting taxi. When the agreed-upon date came and went, Mammaw came to the gripping realization that she had been duped. I am not sure how Mammaw alerted my dad, but he soon arrived in Prichard, Alabama, near Mobile and about an hour's drive from his workplace. Mother and I had just returned to Aunt Wilma's. I stayed to play alone on the front porch while Mother went inside to hang up our coats. Seeing Daddy drive into the driveway, I ran to him at the edge of the porch. He secured me in his arms, quickly put me into his car, and sped away. I remember crying as we drove away. Sadly, not because I was leaving Mother, but because I did not have my new coat.

Mother's next attempt to take me when I was not yet four years old was more traumatic. I clearly remember the vivid details. Again,

Pawpaw was at work. Mammaw was doing her household chores while I played alone in the fenced yard guarded by a collie, Peggy, and Uncle Aubrey's yappy mutt, Penny. A taxicab drove into the long turnaround driveway, and Mother leaped out. She came to the fence, and I ran to meet her. She quickly lifted me over the fence with the two dogs barking, snarling, and lunging. Alarmed by the commotion, Mammaw was soon out of the house, running toward the cab where Mother was positioning me in her lap in the back seat. Before the car door closed, Mammaw managed to get a firm grip on me. She would not let me go even as the driver cautiously tried to drive with the backdoor still open, two sets of hands gripping me, and Mammaw's feet being dragged on the gravel driveway. Mother kept yelling for the driver to go. *Then another act of divine intervention*: Ms. Ima, who was the nearest neighbor living about the distance of a football field away, was alerted by the ferocious barking of the dogs. Ms. Ima had a reputation for being nosy in our close-knit rural community. This time, her meddling was welcomed. When Ms. Ima observed the suspicious presence of a cab accompanied by the noisy disturbance, she ran to the aid of her neighbor. As Ms. Ima approached, Mother realized that she was outnumbered, and she released me to the weary, yet relentless, grasp of my grandmother. When Daddy got word of the snatching of his child in his legal custody and the dragging of his mother by the taxi driver, he again arrived from Jackson as quickly as possible. Mother, along with the taxi company and their driver, was threatened with attempted kidnapping charges.

This event quelled Mother's attempts to see me for about five years. Although I received occasional cards, letters, and always gifts from her on special occasions, I drifted from our bonded mother-daughter relationship.

Daddy's Marriage to Beryl

Dad married Beryl Dunn in 1949. Beryl had been previously married when she was eighteen. Her first marriage was short-lived, but from that brief union came my adored stepbrother, Ron Cooper. When Dad and Beryl married, they lived in a small functional house in Atmore. Two-year-old Ron and I, age seven, spent weekends with them. For the remainder of the week, we lived with our respective grandparents. The newlyweds lived on Dad's Swift Hunter Lumber Company's commissary salary, and they saved Beryl's Vanity Fair wages as a factory laborer. By 1954, they had saved enough to buy a half-acre lot and build a house debt free that they enjoyed together and where they hosted many memorable gatherings for family and friends. Uncle Aubrey worked in the lumber yard at Swift Hunter Lumber Company. He selected and set aside premium boards for the construction of Dad and Beryl's house.

It was at that home on South Carney Street where Dad and Beryl began the tradition of the Robinson family's Thanksgiving reunion. In those early years, the attendance was relatively small. Mammaw and Pawpaw, two of Dad's brothers, Vernon and Aubrey, and their families were always present. Sometimes, Dad's youngest brother, Herman, would come with his family from Mississippi. Often great aunts and uncles from as far away as Mobile and Pensacola would join us. Traditionally, Beryl or Dad would call Atmore police officers and firefighters, who were working on Thanksgiving Day, to invite them to come by during the afternoon to eat and takeout from the smorgasbord of desserts. When both my cousin, Sandra, and I married Owens brothers, Doug and Roger's parents, Theodore and Verta

Owens, attended the reunion every year. They joked that they got to be Robinsons for a day. There were the unforgettable after-dinner family sing-alongs around the piano. Beryl did not sing with us, but she delighted in seeing and hearing everyone make a joyful noise, always making sure "How Great Thou Art," "Whispering Hope," and "What a Day That Will Be" were part of the repertoire. After Dad's death in 1985, the pain of his absence was too great for Beryl to continue hosting the reunion. It was then that Uncle Aubrey and Aunt Eunice began hosting the family gathering at their lakeside home in Bay Minette, Alabama. The tradition, sometimes with sixty attendees, continues at that home now owned and beautifully renovated by their son, Don, and his gracious wife, Thelma.

Small-town Atmore, which would be boring for today's expectations, was a great place to grow up. We had caring neighbors; reliable dentists; doctors; hospitals; a good high school, both academically and athletically; McMurphy's Dairy Bar; grocery markets and clothing stores, both chain and locally owned; and a movie theatre. If we ever thought we needed more, families would make the hourly drive to spend a day in either Mobile or Pensacola. Saturday afternoons brought farm families from a twenty-mile radius to shop and to visit on the sidewalks while enjoying ice cream and cherry-coke floats from one of the three drugstores' soda fountains or popcorn and roasted peanuts from the sidewalk vendors. The tempting outdoor aroma of their wares needed no further promotion. Ron and I, along with other local kids, were entertained by the double-feature western movies starring Roy Rogers, Gene Autry, Cisco Kid, Lash Larue, the Lone Ranger, and others, each with his respective sidekick. Local parents got a real bargain for their quarter per child: ten cents bought three continuous hours of movies and Looney Tunes cartoons. Another dime bought popcorn, and moviegoers, with their last nickel, could enjoy a drink from the concession soda fountain.

Daddy became Atmore's city clerk when the Swift Mill commissary closed. Later, he worked as manager of the Yellow Front Store in Atmore. Yellow Front, based in Arizona, was a chain of general stores, although the Atmore location's principal inventory was that of a grocery market. The job for which Dad is best remembered was his capable management of Whitfield Pickle Company's salt station in Atmore. He seemed to be a perfect fit to interact with local farmers and contract them to plant cucumber acreage. Early in his career with Whitfield, Dad would travel to Louisiana and Texas as a buyer for cucumbers and molasses. During harvest time, farmers lined up with their truckloads of cucumbers to be weighed, graded, purchased, and placed in brine tanks to eventually make their way to dinner tables as a number of delicious pickle varieties. The Whitfields also proudly marketed their popular syrup products under the Alaga label.

Dad used his police scanner as auxiliary home entertainment. On a night of rare below-freezing temperatures, he overheard from police-scanner communications that numerous cars had lost control on a local stretch of road after hitting an extensive icy patch. Serving a small southern Alabama town on the Florida state line, the Atmore officers were in a quandary about where they could find enough salt to resolve the dangerous icy road issue. Dad phoned the police station and offered as much salt as needed. He then met the city trucks at the cucumber brine station and loaded salt on the trucks with a forklift called a "doodlebug." In short order, the accident-prone stretch of roadway had been treated and was safe to travel. Daddy was the town hero!

Ernestine James came early into our lives as Dad and Beryl's part-time cook and housekeeper. She was a vital part of our family for thirty-five years. Ernestine referred to herself as our black mama. And indeed, she was. When Ron and I were young children, Ernestine kept her watchful eye on us. She was fun, loving, and patient. Before Daddy's death, she alerted our family that he was not well. She had observed his bending over in the backyard, coughing, shortness of breath, and holding his chest. Dad had asked her not to tell Beryl, but she did. Ernestine's vigilance resulted in our getting Dad medical help that perhaps bought him a little more time before his fatal heart attack on November 16, 1985.

Uncles and Aunts:
A Caring Family

My dad, Marshall, shared a close bond with his two older brothers. The three of them were born between 1910 and 1915. Herman, ten years younger than Daddy, was adored by the three older brothers, but the age differences defined different levels of mischief. Daddy was lovingly indebted to his brother, Aubrey. The hardships on many families brought on during the 1929 Great Depression and the recovery period that followed compelled many older children to drop out of high school or to delay their education. This difficult decision was necessary because most able-bodied family members were needed to share the workload to keep food on the table and to save the family home, farm, or business from foreclosure. Seventeen-year-old Aubrey, three years older than his brother, Marshall, chose to drop out of school and work so that my dad could remain in school. I remember Daddy's excitement and pride for his brother when the family gathered to celebrate forty-two-year-old Uncle Aubrey's receiving his high school diploma. Uncle Aubrey, along with several other Atmore men who had endured similar sacrifices, earned their diplomas under the Servicemen's Readjustment Act of 1944, commonly referred to as the GI Bill.

When Daddy was graduating, Uncle Aubrey paid for his high school class ring. That treasured ring was passed on to me after Daddy's death. To keep its legacy alive, when Doug and I celebrated our fiftieth wedding anniversary in June of 2012, that class ring was melted, together with Doug's original wedding band and my original wedding band and engagement ring, to create newly designed sets of rings with sentiment for both of us.

Aunt Eunice was a fun-loving soul. There were no dull moments in her presence. I have many fond memories. When she sold Avon, she allowed me, as a child, to have some of her lipstick samples, colognes, and makeup to play dress-up. I later learned when I sold Avon that those samples were not free. On a hot summer's day in south Alabama, Aunt Eunice would make punch for Wayne, Don, and me. The cold beverage was a refreshing treat to slurp down and find sunk to the bottom of the glass chopped fruit that she always added to entice us to drink it all. There is still no dessert that compares to her decadent orange-pecan cake with a crunchy sugar glaze. When Aunt Eunice or whoever made a cake and cookies, all available kids got to lick the bowl. Not really *lick*, but each of us had a spoon, and what a treat it was to savor every drop of the raw batter or cookie dough remaining in the empty mixing bowl. We did not need to worry our pretty little heads about salmonella and such!

Aunt Eunice quietly maintained her affection and appreciation for her friendship bond with Mother that was nurtured when Mother and I, age two, rode the train to Santa Fe to be with Aunt Eunice for the birth of her firstborn, Wayne, in 1944. After my parents' divorce and custody battle in 1946, Aunt Eunice never had contact with Mother again until my parents-in-law's sixtieth wedding anniversary in 1998. In 2002, Aunt Eunice's younger son, Don, and daughter-in-law, Thelma, accompanied Aunt Eunice to Mobile for a doctor's appointment. At the same time, Doug and I were visiting Mother in Mobile, and we arranged a lunch reunion. Aunt Eunice, whose best friends were likely my dad and my stepmom, exhibited her special gift of loving my mother for the impact that Mother had made on *her* life. Christlike, Aunt Eunice could look beyond one's faults to address their needs.

Uncle Vernon was the oldest of the four Robinson brothers. It was he who owned the apparently successful gas station and café in Jackson that was leveled in a 1947 fire. This disaster prevailed upon Vernon's family and Daddy, who worked with him post World War II, to return to the Atmore area. After Pawpaw's death in 1959,

Mammaw gave Uncle Vernon and Aunt Margaret a parcel on the north edge of her five acres. Uncle Aubrey and Aunt Eunice were later given a parcel of property where they built a home adjacent to Mammaw's house on the south side. Uncle Vernon drove a delivery truck for Coca-Cola, and he later drove a bread delivery truck. He died of an apparent heart attack in 1968 while at his job at Fountain Correctional Facility. Uncle Vernon enjoyed his role of being the only male in his family: Aunt Margaret, Gloria, and Sandra. His blind mother-in-law, Annie Wiggins, also lived with them until her death in 1956. When I showed up for frequent visits, Uncle Vernon was outnumbered five to one.

Aunt Margaret was a precious lady: beautiful inside and out. She was my go-to confidant when I needed someone who understood girl talk. Aunt Eunice had no daughters, only Wayne and Donald, and Mammaw was literally entrusted with my life after having raised four rambunctious boys. It was Aunt Margaret who introduced me to Merle Norman makeup when I was fifteen years old. She advised me about lipstick shades and matching foundations to skin tone. I continue to use Merle Norman products to this day in hopes that I will one day be as beautiful as she was. Aunt Margaret was probably also a sounding board when Mammaw needed advice on what was next when raising me. Aunt Margaret's pet name for me was Sweet Thing. She was the *sweet thing* who came to encourage and emotionally lift me on many occasions, most significantly when my mother and military stepfather returned from Europe. Later in this story, I address that traumatic rift with my dad when I wanted to see Mother and my stepfather, Johnny, after their ten-year absence.

When Uncle Herman graduated from the University of Southern Mississippi with his degree in education, Mammaw, Pawpaw, and I traveled by train for the celebration. Another draw to celebrate was to see Cheryl, Uncle Herman and Aunt Frances's firstborn of their three daughters. I felt so grownup when I, alone, got to push Cheryl in her stroller on the sidewalk. My cousins, Nancy and Linda, were also born in Mississippi. Due to the long drive and Aunt Frances's fragile health, the families of the other three brothers did not see Herman's family regularly. With the undertaking to begin school desegregation in the late 1950s, the stresses of being an education administrator compelled Uncle Herman to earn a degree in dentistry. In 1980, at age fifty-five, he suffered pulmonary complications several days after spinal surgery. Sadly, he did not survive. Having grieved the 1968 loss of Vernon, the oldest of her four sons, the death of Herman, her youngest, was the onset of Mammaw's noticeable health decline.

Custody Battle: Round 2

Mother's heart continued to break. By 1950, she had married Johnny, a career noncommissioned officer in the U.S. Air Force. Until her marriage to Johnny, Mother was called by her middle name, Viola. Afterward, Johnny began to address Mother using her first name, Edna. This name change was perhaps a psychological indicator to all, especially Mother, that this was a new beginning. Before his departure on assignment to England, Johnny urged Mother to legally revisit the custody battle. He would assume the legal costs—whatever it took. My low-income maternal grandparents also encouraged their daughter to fight for custody. Mother's parents owned a small farm where they earned their subsistent living with the help of their three still-at-home teenagers and Granddaddy's mule, Rhody, raising crops to provide vegetables for eating fresh in the summer and canned, dried, or otherwise preserved for winter. Granddaddy's hunting in the surrounding woods provided wild turkeys, rabbits, and an occasional deer. Hogs, chickens, and a cow completed the livestock necessary to feed their family. Rhody was also the only means of transportation, mostly to their small, but at that time, bustling farm town of Castleberry and to church every Sunday. Granddaddy Kirkland, a kind World War I veteran, did more than emotionally encourage his daughter to revisit the custody decision. He offered to sell whatever it took, including the farm, to help her with legal expenses. This act of benevolence was an interesting turn referencing their June 26, 1946, letter previously mentioned during the divorce proceedings—the letter that was written by Grandmother Kirkland to Mother's sister, Wilma, in support of my dad.

With financial backing from her husband, Johnny, and the emotional support from her parents and siblings, Mother was empowered and determined to reverse the court's ruling of five years earlier. The 1951 venue was the Clarke County courthouse in Grove Hill, Alabama, where the divorce had been finalized in 1946, and the custody award had been in Dad's favor. The proceedings lasted a few days, probably three. Two of my dad's three brothers and their wives and, of course, my beloved paternal grandparents drove from Atmore to Grove Hill to encourage Daddy and me. The daily trip from Mammaw and Pawpaw's house to the courthouse seemed longer than two hours to me as an anxious eight-year-old wondering if my security with the family I dearly loved was in jeopardy. I was regularly reassured that everything was going to be okay. If true, what was meant by all the whispering and conversations behind closed doors? On one of the three days in the courtroom, I was obviously ill. The judge, observing my distress, asked a member of my Robinson family to remove me from the courtroom and accompany me to the jurors' antechamber, where I rested on a bench for the remainder of that day's proceedings.

Finally, the day of the decision arrived. I was only eight years old, but I could sense Judge Joe Pelham's perception and compassion. Observing the love and care of my father, along with the support of his extended family and my established stability with my grandparents, the judge also considered the agony of estrangement that my mother and her family had endured. With the wisdom of King Solomon, Judge Pelham made the call: my mother would have limited custody of me only during the school break in the summer of 1951. She could not take me out of the state of Alabama, and she must return me on a given date before the start of my fourth-grade school year. My Robinson family was relieved that my dad had retained permanent custody, and my mother's Kirkland family planned to make the best of their time with me during the upcoming summer vacation.

Getting Acquainted with
My Kirkland Family

My first few days with Mother and her parents in Castleberry were perhaps my most traumatic childhood transition. Reflecting, I was probably wondering if I would ever return to Atmore. Too fresh in my mind were the times when Mother had taken me with the promise to return me to my dad's parents—and did not. I wondered if I would see Mammaw and Pawpaw again. Or my loving uncles and aunts? Or my four cousins who were my surrogate siblings? Or my dog, Sandy? Meanwhile, back in Atmore at my Mammaw and Pawpaw's home, they were grieving the temporary void in their lives.

Mammaw liked animals in their place. Dogs were for guarding the property and rounding up the cows. Cats kept the rodent population in check. I loved and played with all the critters, from the soft furry ones to feathered ones and even the creepy crawly ones. Just days before I left with Mother in compliance with the court order, Pawpaw was plowing his garden patch with Mr. Beasley's mule when he uncovered a bed of baby mice or rats. Following at his heels, I quickly rescued the distraught babies. Pawpaw left his plowing and looked in his country general store to find a box and rags to use for bedding. The two of us gently placed my new helpless projects snugly into their new home. Mammaw was okay with this. She felt that her one and only contribution was to find an eyedropper, dilute, and warm some milk so that I could begin feeding the orphans. Mammaw cautioned me to regularly wash my hands with warm water and soap. She assigned a towel to be used only after I held the mice for feeding. Fast-forward a few days, Mother arrived on her court-designated day and interrupted my duties as surrogate mom to the baby mice. While I was in Castleberry, news by way of visiting relatives from Atmore made my heart happy when they told me that twice a day, Mammaw was holding and feeding the rodent babies with an eyedropper. One would need to personally know Mammaw to appreciate what sacrificial love she expressed by this act of mercy.

Mother, Grandmother and Granddaddy Kirkland, Mother's siblings, and their children—they all did everything within their power to comfort me. In addition to regular visits from my maternal cousins, Grandmother invited Ann to visit. Ann, a neighbor's daughter, was my age. She and I bonded quickly, and I began to look forward to visits with my new playmate. Mother was one of the few car owners in Castleberry. Ann could come to play only when Mother could give her a ride from her home, which was too great a distance to walk. Ann often wore a dress that I thought was so pretty. The dress had a solid panel accenting the front and back and patterned fabric down each side. One morning when Ann came to play, Grandmother asked Ann to wear one of my dresses. Ann complied. By day's end, Grandmother, using Ann's dress as a pattern, had sewn from feed sacks a dress for me as much like Ann's coveted dress as possible. I felt so loved, beautiful, and secure in my dress like Ann's.

Faye in dress like Ann's

Food for livestock came in sacks made from solid and patterned cloth. Many farmers' wives accompanied their husbands to the feedstore so that they could choose the sacks they needed for their sewing projects. I own some quilts, made by older female relatives, that bring memories of the times they carefully selected a design and bought a particular sack filled with livestock feed. For many farm folks, going to the feedstore was like a present-day shopping trip to Joanne's Fabrics.

So Ann Benefield was my new friend. For two and a half months, Ann's presence brought stability to my topsy-turvy emotions. After returning to my Robinson family in Atmore in time to start the fourth grade, I thought of Ann from time to time, but we did not stay in touch. Over the years, memories of Ann would come but would soon be dismissed because I had no way to follow up. Then came social media, and I searched. I assumed that Ann was married, but I had no idea what her last name might be.

In December of 2018, the mother of my paternal first cousin's (Gloria) daughter-in-law passed away. While posting my condolences to Leanne's Facebook page, I noticed that the maiden name on the post above mine was Benefield. I sent a private message, and the immediate response was that she was Ann's sister. She was elated, and within days, she had reunited Ann and me by telephone. It was six months later, in June 2019, that Doug and I visited Ann and her husband, Bill, at their home in Pensacola, where Ann and I were reunited in person after sixty-eight years.

Dad and my compassionate stepmom Beryl, whom he married when I was seven, came every Sunday afternoon to visit me in Castleberry. They parked at the end of the long driveway that was lined with huge pecan trees providing welcomed relief from the summer sun. Dad, Beryl, and sometimes my three-year-old stepbrother, Ron, would visit for perhaps half an hour, sharing news of the week about my Atmore connections. Dad would regularly ask me if Mother had taken me out of the state. Once I asked Mother if Selma was out of the state because she often drove me there to visit Johnny's parents. Sometimes, Johnny's son and daughter, slightly older than I, would also be there visiting their grandparents. As his children grew older, they apparently harbored resentment toward their dad and my mother for perhaps the breakup of their family. Since those days in Selma in 1951, I have seen Johnny's children only once at their dad's funeral in 1983.

Kirkland Family Genealogy

Mother was the second child born to Bruner and Jessie. Their first baby was stillborn. The birth order of Mother's seven siblings is Doris, Wilma, Millard, Thelma, Levi, Mary, and Glenda (Glen) Joyce. Aunt Doris and her husband, Alvin Moye, had four children. Betty was seven months older than I, and Virginia was slightly younger. Donnie was a toddler, and Barbara was a lap baby, both too young to romp with us during the summer of 1951 on their frequent visits to our mutual Kirkland grandparents' farm. This bonded my familial ties with Betty and Virginia closer than with any of my other maternal first cousins. As an adult, I have reunited with some maternal cousins at family weddings and funerals. The meetings have been polite but not warm. The cordial tie that bound us as children was too brief and strained during that ten-week summer break when I was eight years old.

My Kirkland grandparents built their house around 1918 and incorporated an existing log house that was built in the 1800s. The floor was high off the ground, providing a sheltered area where we children could walk upright and play underneath the house. There was a huge chinaberry tree providing ample shade for the back porch where adults sat sharing stories while shelling peas and beans. A large arbor supported a trailing scuppernong vine that produced indescribably sweet fruit. I can confirm that an eight-year-old girl could eat a quart of those scuppernongs and never have a tummy ache. No one made peanut brittle as delectable as Grandmother. The peanuts were harvested from the Kirkland farm and cooked with syrup made from their homegrown sugarcane. The candy was more chewy than brittle; nevertheless, it was the best I have ever tasted. The dirt yards were kept grass-free and cleanly swept by a brush broom handmade by wiring together gallberry bush cuttings.

Grandmother's colorful, fragrant flowers grew at the edge of the front porch, where they attracted butterflies, bees, and humming-birds. The flower garden was watered several times daily by emptying leftover water from the communal pan used for washing hands and faces. Drinking and washing stations with buckets filled with water drawn by a rope from the coolness of the backyard well conveniently sat on the front and back porch shelves. Nearby, a shared towel hung on a nail driven into the adjacent wall. Another watering source for yard plants was the residual water slung from the drinking dipper shared by everyone in the household plus any thirsty visitors who dropped by. Other than hit-or-miss rainfall, the well was the only source of water for people and farm animals alike.

Some of my fondest memories with Granddaddy revolve around his hitching his mule, Rhody, to the four-wheel wagon. Granddaddy and I would ride the bumpy, gravel country road seven miles into town, buy supplies, and return home to the shade of the chinaberry tree where we would cut a homegrown watermelon that had been cooled in the well.

The rolling store was a welcomed sight when it arrived on its scheduled day. Its name described it perfectly: a general store on wheels that sold limited staple goods from flour and sugar to thimbles and treats. Mother told me the somber story of my great-grandfather, the Reverend Mark Kirkland. Her Grandpa Mark would often hop aboard the rolling store to ride the route with his friend, the driver. This being a fairly regular practice, there was no undue concern on a late summer evening until Mother's Grandpa Mark did not return to his home at suppertime. Communication with family and neighbors was difficult at best and appeared to be worse during emergencies. A family member rode his horse to the home of the rolling store owner to learn the devastating news that Grandpa did not ride that day. Alarmed, neighbors were notified, and the frantic search began. The next day, Mother's grandpa's body was found where he had become entangled in a fence and had been unable to free himself. Apparently, he had died while trapped for hours in the heat of the August sun. As Mother recounted the story, she grimaced at the memory of her grandfather's parched face when she, at age sixteen, saw him in his casket.

The loss of her maternal grandfather, Andrew Moore Kirkland, was equally traumatic. Mother recounted the story that happened when she was a young child. The setting was a warm December afternoon. Several adult family members sat visiting on the front porch; some pushed themselves back and forth in the squeaky swing while others sat in handmade slatted rockers with seats made from tanned cowhide or deerhide. Some were enjoying a dip of snuff from tins purchased from the rolling store. Cowbells clanged as the milk cows returned to the barn with full udders. Their mooing reminded the milkers that it was feeding and milking time. (My great) Grandpa Moore Kirkland temporarily ignored the bellowing of the cows to finish the "where's-the-penny" game he was playing with Mother, who was six years old. Puzzled, she sat in his lap, carefully watching his sleight of hand as he quickly popped the evasive penny into his mouth. The game ended abruptly when Grandpa Moore Kirkland left the porch coughing. All the family assumed that he had gone to care for the cows. When the cows continued their mooing, someone left to help with the feeding and milking and found Grandpa gasping for breath in the barn, where he later succumbed to choking on the penny. I think Mother felt some burden of responsibility for his death. Occasionally, Mother would become emotional as she relived that tragedy etched in her young memory.

If you, the reader, have noted that Mother's maternal grandparents' and her paternal grandparents' surnames are the same, you are perceptive. Mother's grandfathers, Matthew Kirkland and Moore Kirkland, were brothers. Yes, her parents, Bruner McDonald Kirkland and Jessie Viola Kirkland, my grandparents, were first cousins.

Home Again: My Happy Place

At summer's end, my extended Atmore family celebrated my return with homemade ice cream, watermelon, and boiled peanuts. I was soon back in school and routine: reconnecting with my Robinson cousins, hunting rabbits with Sandy, and picking blackberries with Mammaw.

It was when I was an adult picking and canning blackberries for my own family that I realized the intense work involved not only in picking while avoiding rattlesnakes and chiggers, but also in removing the stems, washing the dust and insects from the fragile aromatic berries, and then canning them to use later for making delicious Sunday dinner cobbler. But Mammaw never complained when I would get off the school bus and sometimes ask for canned blackberries for my snack. She would simply open the pint jar, then sit and talk with me about my day while I sometimes consumed the entire contents of the jar.

The canning process was more difficult in the 1950s when canning was the chief method of preserving food. Today's canning lids have a rubber sealant adhered to the lid and are not reusable. Mammaw would soak her previously used canning jars for hours. Then she would scrub them to remove any remaining rubber sealant from the tops of the jars. After packing fruit, berries, jellies, or vegetables into the canning jar, a rubber seal similar to a thick flat rubber band was meticulously fitted onto the jar rim, carefully held in position while placing the lid, and followed by screwing on the rings. A timed hot-water bath in the speckled-blue enamel canner completed the process and ensured some good eating when winter came.

Soon after returning me to Atmore, Mother departed to join my stepfather, Johnny, in England. She was battle-weary and distraught because she did not have me to accompany her. I began fourth grade on schedule with Miss Ellen Solomon as my teacher at Rachel Patterson Elementary School. My class was Miss Solomon's first after she had received her teaching degree. She was young and pretty, eager to teach, and she made learning fun, but Daddy and Beryl did not like her. When I grew up, I asked Beryl why they did not like Miss Solomon. Beryl's response was that Miss Solomon was too young and immature, and they felt that she was not a good teacher. My speculation is that they did not like her because Miss Solomon allowed me to leave the classroom to go to the school parking lot to visit with my Kirkland-side aunts and cousins. Since they were not allowed to visit me otherwise, my Kirkland family would pack themselves and gifts for me into a car and travel up to two hours from Castleberry, Brewton, and Pollard to my school. Obviously, one can conclude that school *security* in the 1950s was a seldom-heard word, concern, or practice. My relatives would show up unannounced at school and tell the principal, Mr. Garland Butler, that they were my kin. Mr. Butler walked down the hall, called me from Miss Solomon's classroom, told me my aunts and cousins were in the parking lot to see me, and away I went for my perhaps a once-a-month visit. Daddy became aware of their visits when I showed up at home with gifts of games, toys, and teddy bears. He eventually met with Mr. Butler and put a stop to their visits. Sadly, other than that one summer in Castleberry plus the limited school visits, I have never emotionally connected to my Kirkland cousins. Even with access to social media as adults, we seldom interact. In contrast, although separated by distance for our entire adult lives, my Robinson cousins still stay in touch and lovingly fill the innate role as my surrogate siblings.

Many relatives who visited Mammaw and Pawpaw were my dad's generation who dearly loved their Uncle Zollie and Aunt Anna. I became closely bonded to Pawpaw's siblings. I still have my collection of silver dollars given to me, one per visit, from Pawpaw's brother, Uncle Jack. Being the oldest of twelve children, Mammaw had siblings the same ages as her own sons. Consequently, I welcomed the closeness I fostered with my dad's first cousins, several of whom were my age and younger. I was blessed to have had the opportunity to have known two great-grandparents: Pawpaw's mother, Mattie Reaves Robinson (1859–1951) and Mammaw's father, Isham Jordan (1866–1947). In my Kirkland lineage, I likely met my maternal great-grandmother Nancy (Nanny) McCormack Kirkland (1860–1952) in Castleberry during my brief 1951 summer connection to my Kirkland family. Sadly, that summer was a blur. I regret that I don't remember such a significant occasion when I was eight years old.

Isham's father, James (Jim) Ladson Jordan (1846–1920), my second great-grandfather, fought on the Confederate side in the War Between the States. Mammaw (1888–1983), his granddaughter, told me that Jim enlisted in 1861 at age fifteen. He lied to the recruiting officers, telling them that he was the required enlistment age of sixteen. Jim was shot in his leg at the Battle of Marietta in 1864 and received an honorable medical discharge in 1865. According to Mammaw, Jim was slightly lame for the rest of his life. On his way home from the war, Jim limped to the cotton field where his sixteen-year-old sweetheart, Sarah Emmons (1849–1910), was picking cotton. The couple was married that day with Sarah still in her field clothes. Jim's teenage bride, Sarah Argent Emmons, is my link to her great-grandfather Abraham S. Emmons (1760–1821), my fifth great-grandfather, who fought in the American Revolutionary War, also known as the American War of Independence (1775–1783).

My Martinville Community Family: It Did Take a Village

Growing up in the close-knit farm community of Martinville near Atmore was equivalent to having an extended communal family. Family names I recall are Smith, Roberts, Jones, Strawbridge, Lewis, Middleton, Davis, Lancaster, Goolsby, Marshall, Carver, Beasley, Bell, Barnhill, Skinner, Monk, Vickery, Digmon, Terry, Lassiter/King, Bailey, Cotton, Posey, three unrelated Owens families, another Robinson family unrelated to mine, and Buxton. Mrs. Buxton was a midwife who delivered Douglas Owens, who nineteen years later became my husband.

The barter system was a common and acceptable method of payment. My grandparents swapped butter, eggs, loan or gift of tools, or whatever was available to offer in exchange to Mr. Beasley for the use of his gentle mule, Babe, to plow our garden, to Rufus Bell in exchange for digging a well or for pump repair, and to Jim Middleton for "service" of his bull, who conveniently lived in the pasture adjacent to our cow pasture and was always happy to oblige, even on one occasion to the point of tearing down the property-line fence.

Faye sitting on Mr. Beasley's mule

My first puppy love was my infatuation with the fourteen-year-old neighbor, Ray Bell, son of Rufus Bell, a well digger, and his wife, Ella Mae. At age nine, I carefully selected for Ray the most special valentine from the box purchased to share with my fourth-grade classmates at the party planned by our teacher, Miss Solomon. When Ray walked the half mile on Valentine's Day to Pawpaw's store to purchase groceries for the Bell family's daily needs, I shyly handed him the valentine thoughtfully chosen just for him. As Ray reached for the card, a valentine from another suitor fell from his pocket. My heart sank when I saw that my rival had creatively threaded a lollipop through her card, making it much more impressive. One month later, our Martinville community and small town were devastated with the news that Ray had been electrocuted while standing on the rain-soaked ground to work on his plugged-in originally battery radio converted to AC. That tragedy, like others, was viewed as part of life. The community grieved, comforted the families involved and each other, and then pretty much moved on. However, from that Valentine's Day forward, including showing my young daughters how to thread a lollipop through their cards, all valentines for classmates included lollipops and were given as a memorial to Ray.

On a February day in 1957, I was reading during the study period in the auditorium of our Escambia County High School. Mr. Black, our principal, and Mr. Melvin Nall, a staff member at First

Baptist Church and a friend of Doug's family, walked swiftly past my chair and down the aisle of the auditorium. I watched as the two men spoke softly to Doug, who was studying nearby. Doug left the auditorium and returned shortly to gather his books and coat. I sensed some concern about my friend, but I did not learn until I arrived home that Doug and Roger's dad had suffered a serious brain injury while sawing with a circular saw in a local sawmill. The saw struck a sawmill dog, a bracket that held the log in place. The dog had been left ajar after having previously sawed a longer log. The detachable teeth from the saw became projectiles, one penetrating Mr. Owens's skull and damaging his brain. The prognosis was not good. If Mr. Owens survived, he would likely be unable to speak. The community of Atmore gathered to pray and support this family in shock.

Early spring was a critical time for farmers to cultivate their land and plant their crops. Neighboring farmers came with their tractors to help plant the Owens family's 140 acres. With the help of their grandfather, Sherman Owens, Doug, at age fourteen, and his twelve-year-old brother Roger took on the responsibilities of adults to ensure that the fall harvest would be successful in providing their family income. The inherent strength of Doug, his mother, and his younger sibling was challenged to the limit during this trying time as each tried to stay strong for the other two while dealing with their own anxieties and fears. Meanwhile, both children kept up their school attendance and classwork.

Within a few weeks, Mr. Owens began to show signs of improvement. He slowly learned to talk again, although his speech was halting and slow as he struggled. For months, he suffered occasional seizures that prevented his ability to drive. With medication, the seizures were lessened and eventually controlled. By the time of his death forty-two years later, my father-in-law was almost back to normal. Those who did not know about his previous near-fatal accident were unaware of any unusual behavior.

In addition to Doug, there were four boys in Martinville who were my age: Franklin, Jimmy, Bobby, and Roy. With no girls my age in the community, these boys were my playmates. I used the term *playmates* loosely because, at an early age, all of us had home-work during school term and home chores year-round. Any leisure time was a luxury. When Franklin finally mustered up the nerve to ask me to go to a movie, I was surprised and anxious. At age fifteen, this would be my first date. I told Franklin that I would first need to ask my dad. Well, Daddy said he would think about it. By the time Daddy said he reckoned I could go, Franklin had asked someone else.

It was about this time that Onree Owens moved with his family to manage the large dairy farm owned by his mother, Lula, and stepfather, Tom Jones. The now-deceased Mr. Jones was the neighbor who had driven my mother to the hospital when she was in labor. I was pleased to learn that Onree (Mr. Owens to me) had a daughter, Marilyn. Although she was two years younger than I, we quickly developed a friendship and played together frequently. As young teens, we rode our bikes around the countryside and roller skated on the concrete floor of her dad's colossal Quonset barn. Being the only other young girl in the community, I was regularly invited to join Marilyn's family for fish-fry gatherings and other outings. Her grandmother, Mrs. Richerson, lived in the neighboring fishing town of Stockton near the historic Tensaw River. Second to Mammaw, Mrs. Richerson was my favorite cook. I continue to use some of her recipes written in my childhood scribble and now stained with butter and chocolate, identifying them as my go-to favorites over the years.

At some point as teenagers, Marilyn and I decided that we wanted to earn some extra money. We took what we thought would be the easy route and approached her dad, Onree, to work as laborers on his large farm. He assigned us work following behind his potato-digging farm equipment to gather potatoes left exposed on top of the soil. He wisely hired us with the caveat that we would be expected to work the whole day, just as he expected from all his hired hands. We were tired, dirty, and "rich" at the day's end. After a hearty meal prepared by Marilyn's mom, Marie, Marilyn and I, now energized, climbed atop the potatoes and rode five miles on the bed of the partially loaded truck to Atmore's potato shed where the potatoes were sorted and graded. My dad's cucumber-grading and brine station for Montgomery-based Whitfield Pickle Company, founded in 1906, was adjacent to the potato-grading shed. During potato and cucumber season, we shared our small town with an influx of migrant workers from Mexico.

Paul and Merle Skinner were our closest neighbors. Merle's elderly widowed mother, Mrs. Caraway, lived with the family and helped care for Dwayne and his baby sister, Debbie. When in elementary school, Dwayne and I would tie a rope or string, as reins, to a grooved end of long sturdy sticks, and we would pretend that these were our horses. We would gallop all around the pasture and up and down the unpaved Bell Fork Road as we played cowboys/girls, stopping occasionally to feed our "horses" mayhaws and to let the thirsty palomino stick horses have a drink from the two ditches parallel to the bed of the old Carney Mill Company railroad that ran through our cow pasture. In its glory days, railcars carried logs along its route to the sawmill that provided a livelihood for many rural families.

When I was a child, there were occasional community social gatherings typically hosted by the Lewis, Beasley, and Monk families, parents of Martinville's teenagers. All neighbors were invited. The adults sat and talked; the children played hide-and-seek, jump rope, and red rover. The teenagers enjoyed games that would romantically coax likely or unlikely couples during spin the bottle, pleased or displeased, and other similar games. These games gave license to participants to play Cupid and encourage or tease the blushing teens by having them comply by holding hands while going for a walk, dancing, singing a love song to someone, or some similar humorous event. The typical party fare was homemade ice cream, cakes, cookies, candy, and peanuts freshly dug from the surrounding fields and boiled in salty water in a black cast-iron wash pot.

My saintly grandmother was not only a motivator and encourager to our family, but she was also one who reached out to those in our rural community. A few years ago, I attended a reunion of Martinville community residents. One woman shared from her childhood nostalgia. Her family was in dire poverty while her father of six was serving his sentence at nearby Atmore Prison Farm. As a child, she would walk on a hot day the half mile across an open pasture to our house, hopeful that we would have ice to share with her family. We had no transportation to drive her home because Pawpaw drove our only car to work. Mammaw would divide the ice that had been delivered by the iceman to the insulated icebox on our back porch. She would wrap the ice block with newspapers, along with anything else the child could tote. When Mammaw and Pawpaw bought a Frigidaire refrigerator, we always had ice available to share. Pawpaw hired the teenage brothers in that family to help him build a fence around our cow pasture, and he encouraged the boys by paying them well.

There were occasions when lone drifters would come to our house begging for food. Mammaw and I were typically alone during the day, but we did not fear the strangers. The grateful beggar always received a portion of whatever food was in our house. He would be invited to sit on the front steps or underneath the cool shade of the giant oaks to enjoy his meal.

Typically, there was not a lot of excitement "to write home about" occurring in our quiet tight-knit neighborhood. So when the eccentric folk character, Charles "Ches" McCartney (aka Goat Man), drove his rickety iron-wheeled self-contained wagon through Martinville in 1959, there was quite a buzz. The wagon decorated by junk that Mr. McCartney had accumulated during nearly forty years of his journeys was pulled by a team of nine goats with some of the animals behind to push and/or to serve as brakes. The sight to behold passed in front of our house on Highway 11 (now State Highway 21) on one of his travels through the back roads of the South. Our yard dogs were more bewildered about the bizarre sighting than we were.

AKA Annie Oakley:
Marksmanship and Cowgirl

Daddy gave me a BB gun when I was a young teenager. With the gun came all the safety warnings about how to load, aim, and shoot the gun so as to not injure anyone, especially don't "put out" someone's eye. With my rigorous target practice and determination to upstage the neighborhood boys, I disciplined myself to become a marksperson and a gainful hunter of birds and rabbits. Mammaw dressed and made stew from the doves, blackbirds, and rabbits. No matter how few, she tried to oblige.

The blue jays loudly announced their arrival as they perched in the fig-laden trees near our back door and consumed, or with one peck damaged, the ripening fruit. With the exclusion of mockingbirds that Mammaw said were God's favorites, I was allowed to shoot any birds, especially the obnoxious jays. Once, I proudly brought into the kitchen some pesky blue jays shot in the act of devouring the fig crop. Mammaw exclaimed, "Oh, honey, people don't eat jaybirds." When I asked, "Why not?" she said that she really didn't know why, so let's try them. So at least for that one meal, there were tiny morsels of blue jays on the supper table. Memories of the aroma of ripe sugared figs simmering in the cast-iron kettle still make my mouth water and remind me of my contribution by keeping the blue jay population in check. I knew that soon fig preserves would be on the breakfast table, along with freshly churned butter and hot biscuits.

Another function of the fig trees was the makeshift monkey bars that the strong lower branches provided for Wayne and me. We were hanging upside down on those favorite happy places in November 1948 when Mammaw came from the house, drying the dishwater from her hands onto her apron. She excitedly announced to us that Elizabeth II had given birth to baby Prince Charles! We children did not appreciate the significance, but both I, at age six, and four-year-old Wayne joined Mammaw in celebrating the royal event. The three of us, unaware of and unconcerned about any royal protocol, danced in a circle, singing, "Princess Elizabeth has a baby boy!" The princess, age twenty-two, reportedly had been in labor thirty hours before her baby was delivered by caesarean section.

I was ten years old when my fifth-grade class taught by Mrs. Emily Greer was invited to my classmate's (Annette Woodson) home to watch the coronation of Elizabeth II as queen on June 2, 1953. The Woodson family owned one of several local furniture stores and was therefore privileged to be one of the first families in Atmore to own a television. As a sidenote, Annette's mother was the county registrar at Atmore Vaught Hospital, who had recorded the data for my birth certificate.

It was probably a year later before Pawpaw and Mammaw bought our first TV. The closest station at that time was in New Orleans, 200 miles away. Reception was poor, but we didn't know any better, and with the help of an antenna attached to the roof of the house, we enjoyed what we gleaned through the frequently "snowy" screen. Nearby Pensacola and Mobile soon added stations, offering more viewing options with clearer reception. Mammaw and I would rush to wash the dinner (midday) dishes so we could watch "Kids Say the Darndest Things," a segment on *Art Linkletter's House Party* weekdays at one thirty. Mammaw seldom stayed up late to watch, but favorite TV shows for Pawpaw and me were *Gunsmoke, Bonanza, Dragnet,* and the suspenseful episodes of *I Led Three Lives.* On weekends, with no school the next day, Pawpaw and I sat in our rocking chairs and talked while we watched television until the channel signed off at 11:00 p.m. with the playing of our national anthem. It was much later in the 1960s and 1970s that the gripping public announcement was broadcast from television stations across the nation at 11:00 p.m., "The time is eleven o'clock. Parents, do you know where your children are?"

With my dog, Sandy, as my sidekick, I pretended that I was the legendary Annie Oakley participating in Buffalo Bill's Wild West Show. Reflecting, I wonder how we kids survived our rodeos in the pasture where we tried to ride the unwilling young bulls and heifers that we temporarily, but appropriately, named Dynamite, Dagger, and Widow Maker to add to the drama. We would time each other's ability to stay mounted bareback on the animal that seemed to have four hooves in the air more than on the ground.

The most serious injury I incurred while rodeoing was when my persistent yearling scrubbed against the trunk of a tree to rid himself of his equally determined rider. With skin scraped from my leg and causing enough pain that should have received medical attention, Mammaw wisely made the decision that there would be no more barnyard rodeos. The home remedy for my skinned leg was the usual readily available and cure-all turpentine. It was indeed a miracle ointment. With her medicine chest containing camphor, rubbing alcohol, Vick's salve, and turpentine, Dr. Mammaw could treat every pain, wound, and ailment from a stuffy nose to menstrual cramps. Rural farm folks seldom sought a doctor's advice. A pricey and painful dental appointment was scheduled only when a toothache became unbearable and, most likely, the tooth was unsalvageable. The lack of dental preventive care, such as cleanings and fluoride treatments, likely explains why those in my parents' and grandparents' generations wore partial or complete sets of dentures. It was in 1945 that President Harry S. Truman called for the creation of a national health insurance fund. In 1965, President Lyndon B. Johnson signed into law the bill that led to Medicare and Medicaid plans.

Mammaw was stumped and concerned when, as a preschooler, I would frequently complain of a stomachache. None of her home remedies brought relief. I would find some comfort while lying flat under the dining-room table with my bare belly on the soothing, cool linoleum floor. Pawpaw, equally concerned, conferred at work with the prisoners' physician, Dr. Gaines. When Dr. Gaines stopped by our house, he quickly diagnosed stomach worms and treated me with medicine typically given for puppy worms. Very soon, I recovered. From that time forward, I have been pretty much immune to whatever germs and viruses have been sneezed, coughed, or smeared in my direction, including COVID-19 and its variants that is currently, as I write, taking its toll around the globe.

Mammaw and Pawpaw: Godly (Grand) Parents

The local 4-H Club Chapter challenged the rural girls and boys with fun competitive events. The four Hs stood/stands for *head, heart, hands*, and *health*. The mentoring organization engaged and encouraged youth to become involved in home economics and agriculture. Following the traditional mores of the 1950s, boys usually competed by entering a yearling, swine, or poultry in hopes of winning a blue ribbon at the AlaFlora Fair livestock exhibit. One day, I eagerly brought a recipe home from school, along with instructions for baking biscuits for the upcoming 4-H biscuit bake-off. Mammaw's otherwise pleasant face frowned as she read the prescribed recipe. "Facey [her pet name for me], it's time for me to teach you how to make biscuits." I prudently explained that to qualify, all contestants must follow the rules and use the ingredients and methods as instructed. "Well, okay, honey. You go ahead. But you won't win." She was right. I shall never forget that I not only missed winning a 4-H ribbon, but I also missed that opportunity to learn how to bake her mouthwatering light, fluffy biscuits that could float off one's plate.

Even Mammaw's light, fluffy biscuits, churned butter, grits, bacon or sausage, and homemade preserves did not whet my early morning resistance to food. Before bedtime one night, she reminded me of the importance of eating breakfast. Prefacing that she worried when I went to school with little or no food until lunch, Mammaw offered to prepare whatever would entice me to eat. Loving fresh garden vegetables, I suggested butter beans (limas). The next morning, I was awakened by the aroma of corn bread baking, and I sat down to my custom-made delicious butter beans, corn bread, and tomatoes. Mammaw did not need to worry that day that I went to school on an empty stomach.

Mammaw taught me so much about work ethic, cooking, gardening, parenting, and life in general. She learned responsibility early from her loving parents and by virtue of her being the oldest of twelve children. The Jordans were a poor farm family who somehow made a way for their daughter, Anna, to attend Downing Industrial School for Girls that opened in nearby Brewton, Alabama, in 1906. The finishing school provided education in business courses, domestic sciences, and music. Industrial instruction included dressmaking, needlework, laundry, canning, cooking, dairying, poultry raising, and floriculture. When Anna left home to attend Downing, her parents, Isham and Nanny Jordan, gave her a trunk that I now own and cherish. How I wish that the trunk could audibly tell me stories of the treasures and secrets that it has safeguarded over the years. When I was a child, Mammaw would carefully place her layer cakes made from freshly grated coconut into a round hoop-cheese crate that she had salvaged from Pawpaw's country store. The crated frosted cake, surrounded by fresh apples, was then placed inside the trunk, where it mellowed over a few days into a melt-in-your-mouth delicacy.

Likewise, I have fond recollections of my grandfather. Pawpaw was a trustworthy respected gentleman. He was always the same, whether in private or in public. His elders were respectfully addressed with a title. Older black friends and acquaintances were greeted as Aunt or Uncle. A tip of his hat with a slight nod of the head showed respect when he greeted a woman of any race. I know their marriage could not have been perfect, but never in my presence did I ever hear him raise his voice to my grandmother nor to me. Pawpaw often stood in my place at the road on a cold day to await his sighting the school bus top the hill half a mile away. He would then alert me with a wave of his hand that the bus was approaching while I watched from the front door window in the warmth of our home's long entrance hall.

One of my favorite outings with Pawpaw was the occasional visit to the livestock auction. Whether he was buying or selling live-stock was irrelevant. We would go there just for free entertainment of hearing the skilled chant of the auctioneer and the interaction between him and the bidders. A sign displaying the compelling message, "Today is the day of salvation. Tomorrow may be too late," hung behind the auctioneer. Attendants were always in the pen to prod the often uncooperating beasts to ensure a thorough look over for potential buyers. A frequent highlight was when an agitated bull would bolt into the ring, snorting bubbles from his mouth and nose, pawing the sawdust on the pen's floor, and slinging whatever onto the spectators. The absolute best drama was when a local cowboy and rancher Henderson Robinson (unrelated to my Robinson family) brought his Brahma bulls to be auctioned. When the bull bounded out the gates, rip-snorting into the sales pen, he would send the attendants scrambling to the safety of the iron-rail barrier between the spectators and the now agitated bull. Somehow, business contin-ued as usual between the bidders and the auctioneer, unaffected by the auxiliary entertainment.

One day, as Pawpaw and I dropped in impromptu to enjoy a hot dog and watch the auction, a cow and her young calf entered the pen. All was status quo until the auctioneer announced, "Cow *only* sold to the gentleman in the green shirt." Piquing my interest, I watched anxiously as the cow was led away, lowing as she looked back at her bleating calf remaining in the sales pen. Pawpaw looked into my tearing eyes as I questioned why the buyer didn't want the calf. The bidding for the now-orphaned calf slowed to the warning call of the auctioneer, "Going once...going twice." At this moment of decision, Pawpaw stood to get the attention of the auctioneer and shouted the magic dollar amount that, to the shock of both of us, bought us a calf. When we arrived home to inform Mammaw of the new addition to our small family of livestock, she was surprised. We all were. As always, Mammaw made room in her heart and in the barn for yet another orphan.

The name Princess turned out to not be the most appropriate for my new calf. Jezebel would have been more fitting. Princess was a mixed Hereford, a breed raised more for beef than for dairy products that our Jerseys, Bonnie, Nellie, and Molly, lovingly contributed to our family table and supplemented income as several neighbors bought whole unpasteurized milk, butter, and buttermilk. The cackle of the hens from the chicken house proudly announced that they too had made their contribution.

Princess (aka Jezabel) bonded quickly with me. Onree Owens, a neighboring farmer, lived a quarter mile away. He returned Princess home on at least two occasions after she had jumped or pushed through the fence to join his herd of dairy cows. She soon began to trust me and would come to me when I walked into the pasture. I could pet her and feed her, but no one else could get near her. When the time came for Princess to be bred, Mr. Middleton's bull again accommodated. When her calf was born, Princess was still skittish, allowing only me to come close. This meant that I had to rise early, even on school days, to milk her. Princess's Hereford beef-cattle lineage denied her the prestigious title of "milk cow." Her milk (called blue john because its low-fat content gave it a blue hue) did not meet Mammaw's high standard of rich and creamy, and it was not wholesome enough for our family and neighbors. The milk from Princess was, for the most part, used to feed the pets. When my school schedule included a heavier study load plus an after school job at a local department store, Princess was returned to the livestock auction where she had last seen her mother. However, my caveat was that she would not be sold separately from her calf.

Pets

I delighted in the companionship of numerous farm animals and treasure fond memories of my interactions with them. Farm kids and adults as well adjusted to the fundamental inevitability that the destiny of many farm animals was the dinner table. There were no tears, just reality. Mammaw and Pawpaw had two turkey hens and a gobbler. Tom, for a time, was a favorite pet. At age five, I could climb onto Tom's broad, soft feathered shoulders, and he would proudly strut around the barnyard with me on his back. One day, for no apparent reason, Tom suddenly began attacking me. His aggression occurred every time I ventured into his territory. My affection for Tom turned to fear. My grandparents would not tolerate Tom's behavior and his threat to my safety. With November approaching, Mr. Wheeler Crook, owner of the City Café, one of Atmore's family-owned restaurants at that time, offered to purchase Tom to be the featured item on City Café's Thanksgiving menu. My grandparents and I were invited to enjoy free Thanksgiving dinner at the restaurant. Mammaw and Pawpaw were not too sure how I would feel about having a roasted slice of Tom along with my dressing, giblet gravy, cranberry sauce, collard greens, sweet potato casserole, and pumpkin pie. My affection for that turkey no longer existed. The three of us enjoyed a delicious, memorable dinner.

One of my favorite stories is that of a bantam chick given to me so that I could enjoy the novelty of owning a miniature chicken. Even when the biddy grew to maturity, she was dwarfed by the other hens in the barnyard. Still her maternal instincts led her to sit on the infertile eggs in her nest. Mammaw told me that because we did not have a bantam rooster, her eggs would not hatch. I did not understand the implied biology, but I thought it was interesting when Mammaw replaced the bantam's eggs with three fertile duck eggs. Ms. Bantam dutifully hopped onto the nest, and she stretched her tiny wings to the maximum to cover the eggs. She was fun to watch as she sat on and carefully and patiently cuddled the three eggs in her nest for the twenty-eight-day incubation period. Then what a sight to behold! Ms. Bantam proudly came off her nest with her three ducklings, each one almost the size of the foster mom. Ms. Bantam strutted her brood through the barnyard, turning the heads of fowl and mammal alike, as all did a double take of the strange family. The bantam would cluck, and her downy, yellow babies would follow.

Within a few days, a heavy rain left puddles in the shallow ditches. The ducklings were so excited, and they headed straight into the water with Ms. Bantam running as fast as her short little legs would go, trying to warn her babies not to go into the ditch, but to no avail! As the ducklings swam and playfully dunked their heads, their befuddled momma would stick her foot in and then immediately withdraw it. This was one of many similar swims the ducklings enjoyed as they grew and grew and grew until each was huge in comparison to Mama Bantam. Even when the ducklings grew into adulthood, the foursome was inseparable and always fascinating to friends and neighbors. As we observed mama and babies interact over the months, we concluded that the family was bilingual: Ms. Bantam could understand *duck*, and the ducklings, whether they were obedient or not, could obviously understand *bantam*.

To supplement his family's income and protein, Uncle Aubrey raised rabbits in a hutch adjacent to their house in Atmore. I was intrigued when watching and cuddling the little bunnies. With permission from my grandparents (his parents), Uncle Aubrey let me choose one to take home. Jack, with beautiful markings similar to those of a Siamese cat, was immediately welcomed and assimilated by the farm dogs and cats. He had complete freedom and would safely hop outside at will and was never confined to a hutch. In addition to his own food pellets, Jack shared meals from the dogs' dishes that contributed to his growth into a large buck. Seventy years later, I still bear the tiny horseshoe-shaped tooth-mark scar on my forearm, a permanent souvenir of the time I sneaked up from behind and grabbed him. Frightened, Jack fought back in defense. Often spending time inside our general store, the large free-roaming rabbit was a novelty to customers. Then came the anxious days that turned into weeks and finally to our acceptance that Jack was gone indefinitely. Mammaw was always suspicious of one of our store customers, whom she thought had abducted Jack.

Of all my childhood pets, Sandy was my most dear. From the time I was five when Sandy was born until the Easter Sunday morning eleven years later when he was struck by a car, he was my buddy. It was Sandy's mother, Penny, who, along with Mammaw's collie, Peggy, alerted our neighbors of Mother's earlier-mentioned kidnapping attempt. Sandy was always my shadow, whether he was retrieving sticks, chasing Jack, or nuzzling my arm when my head was buried in my hands grieving Pawpaw's death. Our favorite place to play outside was underneath the huge pecan tree in the cow pasture where Pawpaw had hung a swing that, with momentum, I felt that I could get high enough to kick the fluffy clouds. When the thunder warned that a rainstorm was imminent, Sandy and I would race to safety and curl up on sacks of aromatic cow feed in the back of Pawpaw's store.

Following Sandy's tragic death, I was given a mix-breed black Labrador and German police puppy, whom I named Lady. She was a descendant of neighbor Tom Jones' dog, Smokey, whom I had feared for years. Lady was beautiful, intelligent, a fierce protector of Mammaw and me, and a loyal companion. When Doug and I married, I left Lady with Mammaw. I felt secure that Mammaw, now alone, was safe under Lady's watch. When Lady fell terminally ill, her verdict was that of other predecessor pets. Uncle Aubrey came with his rifle from his house, now next door to Mammaw, to "put Lady out of her misery."

Lacking the weather-tracking technology currently available, intense weather systems often caught us off guard. Sometimes, the summer storms, fueled by the Gulf of Mexico's heat and humidity, produced wind, hail, flooding, and lightning. Power outages were common occurrences. No worries. My grandparents would call the skilled and reliable Rural Electric Association's (REA) repairman, Henry White, who usually arrived quickly to survey and repair the damage. On one anxious occasion, the electrical wire had been severed and was now lying exposed across the wire fence between our house and Pawpaw's store. Mr. White stood puzzling over this quandary. He warned all of us to stand back until he could determine whether the wire was live and could possibly electrocute anyone or any living thing that touched the fence. While we cautiously kept our distance, my precious kitty began walking from the house to me with the potentially hot fence in her path. Hearing Mr. White mumble under his breath, "Uh, oh," I began screaming, "No! No! No!" which apparently incited the frightened cat to run toward me rather than away. One could hear a pin drop as the kitten crawled over the downed wire and safely through the fence. A corporate sigh of relief was heard as I cuddled my kitty, and Mr. White confidently grabbed the bare wire and quickly moved on to his business of safely getting the lights back on.

Elementary School Days:
Maxwell and Rachel Patterson

Not only did Mr. Beasley participate in bartering by loaning his mule, Babe, to his neighbors, he also drove the school bus, transporting students from our neighborhood and adjacent communities along the route to Maxwell School, Canoe Elementary, Rachel Patterson Elementary, and Escambia County High School in Atmore. Maxwell School was a three-room elementary school located in the rural community of Robinsonville, named for my Robinson ancestors who settled the virgin forest area around 1895. The school building housed two grades in each classroom and included a kitchen where Mrs. Bozeman cooked for those who did not bring a bagged lunch from home.

Maxwell School was built in the Robinsonville community on property donated by the parents of Robinsonville (Atmore) native, WWI Second Lieutenant William C. Maxwell. In 1922, the United States Department of War named Maxwell Field (now Maxwell Air Force Base) in Montgomery, Alabama, to honor the memory of Second Lieutenant Maxwell. At age twenty-seven and stationed in the Philippines in August 1920, Second Lieutenant Maxwell was attempting a forced landing due to engine trouble. He was compelled to quickly abort the landing to avoid children playing in the field of tall sugarcane where he was attempting to land. By doing so, Lieutenant Maxwell clipped a flagpole, crashed his plane, and was killed. Second Lieutenant Maxwell's grave is located in the

Robinsonville Baptist Church cemetery along with many of my Robinson and Jordan ancestors.

A few days before Thanksgiving, Mammaw had looped a string over the neck of an unsuspecting lizard that had been enjoying the warmth and the smorgasbord of persistent flies on the outside screen door. Mr. Lizard was gently placed in a shoebox with leaves and twigs so that I could take him for show-and-tell with my second-grade classmates. Proactive Mammaw cautioned me on the morning that school was to dismiss for Thanksgiving break that I should bring Mr. Lizard home so we could be sure he had food and water over the holidays. When the school day ended, the school bus was quickly loaded with rowdy students eager to get home for Thanksgiving break. About a mile from school, Mr. Beasley looked through his rearview mirror and seeing that I was crying, he asked, "What's wrong with Faye?" When one of the older kids yelled back, "She forgot to bring Mr. Lizard home," I was embarrassed to even more tears as the bus erupted in laughter. Mr. Beasley stopped the bus and came back to my seat to learn more about my plight. I told him, through tears, that Mr. Lizard would likely starve over Thanksgiving. The bus was promptly turned around and headed back to the school. Lamar Bell, one of the older popular boys, hopped off the bus, ran into the classroom, and returned with Mr. Lizard to a busload of cheers! Mr. Beasley and Lamar were two of many *just* folks who, even in simple stresses, stepped up to make a difference in my life.

Directly across the lightly traveled road from Maxwell School was Fore's Store. The family-run convenience stop was similar to Pawpaw's store in that Mr. and Mrs. Fore sold staple goods and fuel to their agricultural community of Robinsonville. One could purchase various candies, sodas, and ice cream that tempted us school kids. In those carefree days, we were free to go at will across to the store before and after school to buy a treat or a guinea pig. In a pen underneath a shade tree were cute little rodents scurrying around on the ground. The sign on the fence advertised that a guinea pig could be purchased for twenty-five cents. Asking my grandparents if I could *please, please,* have one, I was given permission and a quarter. When the next school day ended, I went immediately to the store to choose my new pet before Mr. Beasley's school bus arrived. Mrs. Fore placed Squeaky securely in a box for me to take him home. I loved my new little furry friend. I took care to feed and water him daily as I had agreed.

On the Fourth of July 1950, my aunts, uncles, cousins, and grandparents returned from our annual celebration picnic at nearby Pig Branch. The cool waters of the creek and the anticipation of homemade ice cream when we arrived home helped us tolerate the day's sultry heat. As we drove past Squeaky's cage to unload the cars, my seven-year-old heart pounded. With the excitement of the day, I had forgotten to water my little pet that morning. I frantically ran to his pen to see if Squeaky was okay. He was not. Squeaky had died apparently from the extreme heat and lack of water. To this day, not an Independence Day comes without the sad memory that my negligence caused the death of my guinea pig. I was not scolded nor made to feel guilty by anyone. Quite the contrary, I was the recipient of love and sympathy from my family as they consoled me in my grief. My cousins and I buried Squeaky later that day with a celebration of his life. That was one of many days when I felt compassion and support, and I realized the significance of being part of a caring family.

A few days later, Mammaw peered over her spectacles from the front-porch swing where she sat shelling butter beans. She smiled as Sandy and I were having a tug-of-war competition with a frayed garden rope. Now that Sandy did not have to compete with Squeaky, he enjoyed most of my attention and affection. I got right to the point: "Mammaw, will Sandy go to heaven when he dies?" Mammaw paused to collect her thoughts and, with her bottom lip extended, puffed the gnats from her face. Like taking one's first step, this method to dispel annoying gnats is a fundamental skill acquired early in life among toddlers living in the gnat belt.

"Honey, take a look around us here. Smell those wisterias. See the honeybees and butterflies pollinating our pear tree. Listen to the mockingbird's song. See those white clouds that look like sheep darting across the blue sky. The Bible tells us that God made all these and Sandy for our pleasure, for our enjoyment. Even with the wonders of all God's magnificent creation, the best was yet to come when He

61

created all people in His image. That means He gave only people a soul so we can always know His presence. We can talk to Him in our prayers, and we know that He is listening. Yes, people are God's most special masterpiece. God sent Jesus from heaven to ensure that there was a plan for everyone in the world who believed in Jesus to have a way to and a forever home in heaven. God made everything else for our enjoyment, but He made people for His enjoyment and to be His best friends. The Bible is God's instructions to us. In those instructions, He tells us, 'If you confess with your mouth Jesus is Lord, and if you believe in your heart that God raised Him from the dead, you will be saved.' So because animals are not capable of making that decision, I believe that only people will experience the magnificence of heaven." Reacting to my obvious disappointment, Mammaw's profound closing statement was that heaven is a place of continuous joy with no tears nor sadness, and whatever is needed to make us happy will be there. This satisfied me and left me hopeful that perhaps that heavenly happiness would include Sandy. One year later, I accepted that invitation to follow Jesus for the rest of my life. *Without a doubt, that has been the most important decision of my life.*

Dresses or skirts were the dress code for girls throughout my twelve years of school. On the one declared "snow day," the unexpected light snow fell during the day when students were already at school. The phenomenon was similar to a heavy frost, but even more thrilling than the snow was the principal's announcement at day's end that girls could wear pants on the following day.

During the school year, students would occasionally be advised when a surplus of state-distributed tomato or orange juice, and sometimes cheese, would be delivered to our school. Typically, a note would be attached with a safety pin to the child's clothing to deliver a message to the parents. Likewise, this was the method used by parents to communicate with the teacher. On the day following the announcement, students would bring a cup or glass from home to enjoy the free beverage or cheese. There were provisions for those who forgot or didn't have a container, so no one was denied the treat.

The county's health mobile would make its annual rounds to elementary schools where nurses would scratch arms to test for tuberculosis, give vaccinations, and hand out *Hubert the Hookworm* children's books. Hubert's story was captivating but scary, as it warned children and parents about the hazards of going barefoot on the farm. Reading the book annually and adhering must have kept all of us safe. I never knew of anyone who had hookworms.

Doug (my husband since 1962) and I were in the same first/second-grade room at Maxwell School with Mrs. Mazie Ray as our teacher. The state age requirement was to be six years old before September 30 to enroll in first grade. Maxwell School somehow came in under the radar because I, along with several of my classmates, including Doug, did not meet that prerequisite. I transferred to Rachel Patterson in Atmore for third through sixth grades so that I could have access to a piano teacher. I had become quite gifted at picking out a melody by ear on the piano. Mammaw convinced Daddy to encourage me in my interest in music by paying for piano lessons. Mrs. Williams, wife of Atmore's postmaster, was my piano teacher. Mammaw was the one who actually taught me piano techniques as she helped me practice each week and prepare for recitals during my five years of lessons. Best of all, Mammaw encouraged and allowed me to be *me*: a tomboy Annie Oakley who could shoot a BB gun, ride in a rodeo, and milk cows. She also taught me to love literature, poetry, music, and how to display the charm and elegance of Emily Post when fitting for the occasion.

During the 1950s, air-raid drills at schools and public institutions were as routine as fire drills. We students knew, at the sound of the alarm, to take cover underneath our desks, pull our knees up, lower our heads, and roll into a ball as tightly as we could with one arm behind our neck. Sturdy building structures throughout communities were designated as bomb (or air-raid) shelters. I do not recall that the drill was emotionally disturbing. We knew what to do if at school and where to go if in the community, so life's activities continued with little stress, drama, or interruption. Similarly, when we lost school friends, whether because of natural health issues or, as in one incident, tragically shot, we grieved, learned to cope with our loss, and then moved on with parental and peer support. School counselors were trained and available to offer academic advice but not emotional support. My wise Mammaw's response after listening to my heartbreaking stories was a kiss of assurance on my forehead and advising, "Okay now, honey, we will get through this," and then she would try to lead me emotionally to a happier place.

Another naivety was how my classmates and I flippantly handled the seriousness of government-issued dog tags. When the Cold War escalated to potential combat, all students were issued dog tags to wear for identification in the event our bodies were discovered following a nuclear/atomic bomb attack. Teenage sweethearts were soon exchanging their dog tags to seal their puppy-love commitments.

A Little Mischief

My grandparents enjoyed life, and they taught me how to live, laugh, and love. No one under their roof dared to moan, grunt, complain, or scream unless the house was on fire or someone was in a life-threatening situation. The response was that the offender was given a chore to distract from the perceived problem or "Get a drink of water, and then see if you feel better." To spice things up, both of them loved a little occasional self-generated mischief.

A typical Saturday was spent in preparation for Sunday: getting church clothes ready, cleaning the house and yards, and prepping for Sunday's company dinner. I was fascinated as I watched Pawpaw wring (break) the chickens' necks for Sunday's dinner menu. The bird was deceased within minutes, then placed in a bucket where scalding water was poured over him to loosen the feathers, especially the hard-to-remove pinfeathers. As gruesome as one may think, I closely observed the technique and was ready to literally try my hand at wringing the fowl's neck. Reaching into the coop where Mammaw kept the chickens destined for the dinner menu for a few days to "clean them out," Pawpaw pulled out a chicken for my first death-row attempt. I realized that my grip or snap of the wrist was not as strong as his when the supposed-to-be-dead Rhode Island red hopped up, shook it off, and immediately joined the other look-alike fowl in the chicken yard. Pawpaw urged me to catch the escapee and try again. I replied that I would surely be in trouble with Mammaw because I did not know which chicken had been grain-fed while awaiting his doomsday. Pawpaw's eyes twinkled as he laughed and said, "Just go catch one. She won't know the difference!" So with the selection of the scapegoat accomplished, and with my tiny hand firmly gripping his neck, with great determination, I squeezed and twisted and squeezed and twisted until the headless chicken fell flopping to the ground, the rest of his anatomy still in my hand. On Sunday, Pawpaw sat down at the food-laden dining table, winked, and smiled at me as we and our guests discussed family, church, community, and farming while savoring that delicious southern-fried chicken.

As far as I know, Mammaw never knew about that cover-up, although I came very close to confessing the day that she and I were cooking in the freshly painted kitchen, a chore that Pawpaw had finally gotten checked off his honey-do list. Distracted by other meal preparation, Mammaw and I left a pan of hot grease unattended until we saw flames leaping from the pan above the stovetop and onto the newly painted wall. Thankfully, the only damage was the scorched yellow wall just above the stove. Before Pawpaw arrived home that evening from the Atmore Prison Farm, where he worked as kitchen cook supervisor, my creative Mammaw and I had found a partially used can of paint and added yellow food coloring, plus any other tints, until it was amazingly close to the right shade. We meticulously painted the scorched area and cleaned up all the evidence. It was Mammaw who giggled and winked at supper that night. I think Pawpaw knew because that wall never again looked quite right. I do think, however, that whenever he was suspicious about the wall, he remembered the conspiracy behind that tasty chicken dinner that had recently adorned our Sunday dinner table.

My Childhood Churches: Bethel, Robinsonville, and Brooks Memorial

When Pawpaw worked at the prison farm, he needed our only car to drive the five miles to work. He regularly worked on Sundays, leaving us with no transportation. Although the family's denominational preference was Baptist, Mammaw and I could walk the short distance to Bethel Methodist Church. Doug and I were in the four-year-old beginner Sunday School class together. Both of us remember that our teacher, Mrs. Vickery, gave us take-home cards with a Bible story on one side and a relevant picture on the flipside. As a result of that class connection, Doug was invited to my fifth birthday party.

My celebration was shaded by the backyard oak trees at Mammaw and Pawpaw's house while my cousin, Wayne, celebrated his third birthday with a party in the front yard. Having missed the family classes on etiquette until now, when I opened Doug's greeting card with a dollar folded inside, I disappointedly asked him where my present was. Aunt Eunice quickly intervened by saying, "Oh, honey, money is a very special gift. We will take you to town where you can shop for anything you want!" So for the moment, all was fine; however, when the party was over, Mammaw and Aunt Eunice told me that what I had said to Doug was rude. I should have been more polite and thanked him for the thoughtful gift. I wasn't really scolded, but I was embarrassed. I do remember thinking that I didn't like Doug very much. It was because he didn't bring me a tangible present that I was scolded. Little did I know that in fourteen years, I would be marrying this gentle man and, may I add that, I have been delighted when he has since given me money for any special occasion.

When Pawpaw retired from his job at the prison, he was home on Sundays. Now with transportation, we drove to Robinsonville Baptist Church for the next year or two. The community of Robinsonville was named for Pawpaw's father, John (Jack) Alexander Robinson and Jack's brothers, who had moved from Monroe County (Alabama). My grandparents, Zollie Coffer Robinson (Pawpaw) and Anna Pate Jordan (Mammaw), also a resident of Robinsonville, were married in Robinsonville Baptist Church on January 21, 1910. They are now buried side by side in that church cemetery, along with many of my Robinson and Jordan ancestors.

During the year or so that we attended Robinsonville Baptist Church, I had the opportunity to bond with many of Pawpaw's cousins, who were still part of that church's membership. As a child, out of respect for my distant adult cousins, I addressed them with some abbreviated title for "cousin," which sounded like *Cud'n Lula* (Kilpatrick), *Cud'n Gertrude* (Reaves), and *Cud'n Alvin* (Helton). One Sunday evening before worship service, the adults were visiting outside the church underneath the massive oaks. Nearby, I entertained myself by playing with an amiable frog until Mammaw called to me that it was time to go inside to sing hymns. I always enjoyed the music, but I was usually bored when the message began. I was prepared for that evening's message. I reached into my little purse, and there quietly waiting, wrapped in my handkerchief, was my friendly frog. On our pew, there was every reaction from gasps to giggles. Mammaw calmly walked me outside, where the frog was gently released. My frog did not bring the fame, notoriety, nor royalties that the Mississippi Squirrel Revival grossed for songwriter and country music legend Ray Stevens. Nevertheless, it was a story that I never outlived.

I do not know the reason that Mammaw, Pawpaw, and I left the close fellowship and family connections of Robinsonville Baptist Church and started worshipping at Brooks Chapel in Atmore. The

Brooks Chapel congregation was growing under the leadership of a dynamic young pastor, Bob Cook. At age five, I patiently played with my toys and dolls on the floor of Mr. Northrup's house through hours of planning meetings for the building, chartering, and naming the new place of worship. Had I been older, I would have been a charter member of Brooks Memorial Baptist Church, built in 1950 on North Trammel Street. Brooks Chapel, subsequently Brooks Memorial Baptist Church, was named in memory of Reverend R. W. Brooks, a retired minister born in 1852. Rev. Brooks had the distinction of not only being a successful pastor in Mississippi, Florida, and Alabama, but he was also a justice of the peace, railroad agent, express agent, postmaster, editor, and writer.

I looked forward to going to church. The adults at Brooks Memorial cared for and about me and the other children and teenagers. Their love was demonstrated by their involvement in teaching us, setting positive examples, and providing abundant goodies for frequent social events. I learned at an early age that *the* church was *my* church and not just for the adults. This inclusiveness launched me with a lifetime desire to serve and share my faith. The church's leadership provided a sound doctrinal foundation, for which I am grateful. I can now cope, mostly unshaken, within the current climate of spiritual instability. When eight years old, I joyfully made my public decision to follow Jesus and to accept Him as my Savior and Lord. Soon after, Pastor B. A. Lambert baptized me by immersion. It was about that time that I debuted my solo, "I'd Rather Have Jesus," in worship service ("big church"). Those lyrics have sustained my commitment and remained my testimony. I have stood, sometimes climbing, sometimes clinging, but always lifted, on the shoulders of members of loving congregations of *just* folks.

I was fourteen when Elvis made his third and final appearance on the *Ed Sullivan Show*, Sunday, January 6, 1957. Like every teenager, especially the girls, I wanted so much to see that performance. That Sunday morning before Sunday School, we teens, called Intermediates to designate our church age group, planned how we would persuade our parents (grandparents in my case) to let us stay home from our youth choir practice, worship service, and even our favorite "afterglow" fellowship that followed the evening service. If needed to press our petition, we could say something churchy like Elvis is going to sing "Peace in the Valley." My best opportunity came just as we were finishing our Sunday dinner and recapping the events of our being in church that morning. I went straight to the point. "My friends talked about how Elvis is going to be on the *Ed Sullivan Show* tonight. He is going to sing 'Peace in the Valley.' All [somewhat exaggerated] my friends are going to get to stay home just this once to watch him. May I, please?" There was total silence for what felt like forever. Mammaw and Pawpaw seemed to answer *no* at the same time as though they had also rehearsed their script. I was a little pouty when I showed up for youth choir that evening. I was uneasy and somewhat embarrassed that I would likely be the only one there. I discreetly opened the choir room door and peeked in. I believe I saw everyone present and equally sulking in his or her chair. Then we all laughed. Though disappointed, our youth group learned an invaluable lesson from our parents about the importance of priorities and commitment to our responsibilities. We realized that each parent had independently made the call in the interest of his or her child. The bitterness of the pill was easier to swallow when throughout the following weeks, we saw numerous televised replays of Elvis's performance.

My before-church Sunday chore was to sweep the floors while Mammaw put the finishing touches on Sunday dinner, which was almost always shared with family or friends. Interestingly, Pawpaw would often swap his weekly shoe-shining job with me for my sweeping job. I never quite understood why he would rather sweep. After paying me fifty cents for the shoeshine, the three of us dutifully filled out our tithe envelopes, marking the appropriate boxes indicating if we were Present (10%), On Time (10%), Studied Lesson (15%), On Program (15%), Study Course (10%), Daily Bible Reading (15%), Attending Worship (10%), and Giving to Church (15%). I took that accountability check seriously. Those reminders remain as priorities for both Doug and me. Since our teenage marriage, we have always committed to give at least a tithe (10 percent) of our gross income to our church. God has blessed that commitment.

Pawpaw's General Store

After he had retired from the prison farm in 1948, Pawpaw built the store himself on our property on what was then Highway 11, now State Highway 21. I often think of Pawpaw's store as a forerunner of the 7-Eleven chain. I enjoyed many fun times with my grandparents and neighbors in that community gathering place. When I think of the store, the nostalgic aroma of cow feed seeps into my nostrils. I do not remember if the colorful sacks were stored there for resale or for our own cows' consumption, but the smell was sweet when I made my temporary bed on top of the sacks while waiting for my grandparents to checkup and balance the day's receipts, restock the shelves, and close the store. My responsibility was to manually turn on the gas-pump lights at dusk and off at closing time. In the darkness, the lighted globes atop the gas tanks indicated to passing traffic that the store was open for business. The Texaco gas pumps had pencil-sized holes in the side so that when the eraser end of a pencil was inserted, the internal switch was tripped. Inside the store, a glass candy display case tempted customers with Baby Ruth, Almond Joy, Snowballs, Hershey bars, Payday, Butterfinger, 3 Musketeers and choices of Wrigley's chewing gum flavors. Regularly, and especially during the busy August and September cotton-picking season, I was entrusted at a young age with stocking the candy case and managing the candy sales to customers who had a sweet tooth.

Survivors of the 1929 Great Depression, Mammaw and Pawpaw were generous, yet frugal. Any outdated edibles from the store with any potential of being salvaged found their way to Mammaw's kitchen, where she did her magic to turn into delectable dishes what would have likely been discarded by today's "sell-by" standards. Mammaw would carefully and thoroughly remove the negligible mold from hoop cheese and even link sausage to reclaim the food for our family's consumption with the general understanding that what didn't kill us made us stronger.

Cotton picking in August and September was an especially busy time. The school year always began the day after Labor Day to give students, most of whom lived on a farm, time to help their families pick cotton and harvest the fall crops. Those were the years when cotton was king before later losing some of its clout to more profitable crops like soybeans, wheat, and, more recently, peanuts. Many local farmers picked up and dropped off the predominantly black cotton pickers at a designated location in the black community that white people called "the quarters." Pick-up time was early so that picking the cotton could be more productive before the south Alabama midday sun seared the shadeless fields with intense heat. The pickers dragged a canvas cotton sack behind as they plucked the white puffs. The length of the sack was sized somewhat to accommodate the height of the respective picker. Laborers "weighed in" when their sacks were too full or too heavy to drag. At day's end, the weary pickers were supposedly paid the agreed-upon price per pound for the tallied total pounds picked, and the cotton harvest was hauled by the farmer to Currie's Gin, Atmore Truckers' Association Gin, or Robinson's Gin operated by Pawpaw's brother, William Thomas Robinson (my great Uncle Will). There, the cotton was ginned to remove the seeds and then baled. A sample of the ginned cotton was taken to grade for the color and length of the fiber. Farmers were paid based on the quality and quantity of their baled cotton that was then shipped to cotton mills to be spun into thread for weaving into cloth.

One of my favorite memories was our interaction with the cotton pickers when farmers would bring them to our country store, where the pickers would buy their lunch. The oak trees provided welcome shade and occasionally a refreshing breeze where the tired laborers ate their meals and rested before boarding the backs of the trucks to head back to the fields. In addition to our providing free drinking water, some bought cold soda pop from the Coca-Cola box that was half filled with ice water cooled by electricity. Mammaw bottled pints of cold freshly churned buttermilk and sweet (whole) milk that we sold for five and ten cents, respectively. I would set up the milk stand in the shade of the impressive oaks, and I was allowed to keep the profits although Mammaw had done all the work. I was reminded on Sunday mornings to give 10 percent of that income in my tithe envelope. Milk was a favorite for the cotton pickers probably because it was nutritious and provided more nourishment for the demands of the remainder of the workday. Other popular lunch choices purchased at our store were hoop-cheese wedges, bologna, tins of Vienna sausage, potted meat, or sardines to complement a single-sleeve quarter-pound box of saltine crackers.

I was around twelve years old when I made friends with the black girls in their early teens who had come for lunch from the cotton fields. My new friends and I looked forward to playing around our five-acre farm when they had finished their lunches and when I had fulfilled my duties to help with the lunch rush. We usually climbed to the galvanized tin roof of our barn that was covered with pine straw. It was there that I proudly learned the technique of braiding by placing the tip of the three-needled pine straw between my teeth and, with their instructions, wove the straws into a work of art.

Mammaw was a kind, sensitive soul living in the Jim Crow era. She told me that if I needed to use the bathroom when playing with my black friends, I should go to the outhouse just as the Negroes did instead of using the indoor bathroom. I was comfortable using the outhouse, as instructed, if I could not wait until the potty curfew ended. Like my grandparents, I sensed at an early age the racial discrimination around us. Most whites were decent folk trapped in a culture that was hard for both races. White people with the courage to speak up were sometimes intimidated or otherwise harassed. Although I never saw any evidence of the Ku Klux Klan (KKK) nor was I aware of their activities in our small town, when I was an adult, I heard from reliable sources that the KKK existed. I should not be writing this in past tense as though similar injustices do not currently exist.

The only option to purchase anything locally, whether a quart of milk or a new living room suite, was by cash, check, or bartering. An order from the Sears, Roebuck & Company catalog was accompanied by a personal check or money order. The general purchase policy for small businesses around town was cash and carry. Pawpaw's caring heart for neighbors who could not pay for basic goods impressed him to allow those customers to buy on credit by signing a running tab for their purchases until their payday. When he closed the store after about seven years of operation, two or three customers still owed him apparently enough to merit a couple of drives of twenty miles or so into northwest Florida to try to collect. When Pawpaw and Mammaw saw the poverty of one family on the first trip, the second trip a week later was to take vegetables, meats, and dairy products from our small farm, along with forgiveness for their debt.

After he closed his store in 1955, Pawpaw missed the interaction that he had enjoyed with friends and neighbors who came to chat and shop and with strangers who stopped for gasoline as they traveled Highway 11. When a job opening as a shelf stocker and clerk became available at John McKenzie's plumbing store in Atmore, Pawpaw was hired at a meager wage. He loved his job, and he worked proudly and diligently for a few years as though he were the company president.

Pawpaw's Final Earthly Days and Funeral

A couple of years prior to Pawpaw's death, Doug's family, along with my grandparents and others, had cooperated with the Owens family's downtown First Baptist Church of Atmore to begin a mission church in our Martinville community. The mission church initially met in an abandoned house that stored a few bales of hay. Baptisms were in the cold waters of nearby Sizemore Creek. Young pastors, Wayne (Barbara) Upton and Gill (Helen) Watkins, drove the nearly 400 miles roundtrip each weekend from New Orleans when Wayne and Gill were students at New Orleans Baptist Theological Seminary. Both families continued their respective pastorates with the Martinville congregation after graduating from the seminary. A church building was erected on land donated by Ernest Robinson, unrelated to my family and not connected in any way to the congregation other than being a benevolent resident of Martinville. Nathan Little and his wife, Etta, locals from Atmore, were effective as our dedicated youth leaders.

At age fourteen, Doug and I worked well together to plan programs and activities to encourage unchurched teenagers to attend. We helped to build a core youth group of Martinville young people. Mammaw enlisted Doug to lead congregational singing. She also encouraged Doug and me to sing together. Our favorite duet was "The Love of God," and it has remained our signature song throughout the years. I played piano occasionally when Mammaw was overloaded with other responsibilities and could not play. Doug's parents faithfully kept their promise to take Roger, Doug, and me into Atmore on Sunday evenings to our respective churches so that we could participate in their well-organized youth programs. At some undetermined moment in time, neither Doug nor I felt the need to return on Sunday evenings to our separate churches in town to attend the afterglow social functions. Our friendship was indeed moving to a new level.

Pawpaw's health began to fail when I was fifteen. Our first alert was when in his sleep one night, Mammaw was awakened when his light snoring became a gurgling struggle to catch his breath. Rushing to his bedside, we observed that he was unresponsive. Mammaw panicked. Trying to keep my composure, I quickly flipped through the small-town phone directory to find the number of Atmore's Greenlawn Hospital. An ambulance was immediately dispatched into the five-mile darkness of the country highway. Keeping calm, I provided the dispatcher with the precise rural location and advised him that I would turn on the front-porch light. There were no house numbers for identification. With help on the way, I then phoned my dad and Beryl and Uncle Vernon and Aunt Margaret. They lived near the hospital and promptly drove there to meet the ambulance. At age fifteen, I did not have my driver's license. I felt somewhat at risk with distressed Mammaw behind the wheel, but we safely made our way to the hospital, silently preparing ourselves for the sad news. Pawpaw soon recovered and returned home, only to succumb to a similar recurrence within the year. Recent awareness of sleep apnea and its symptoms takes me back to those mysterious noises associated with his two admittances to the hospital. Had Pawpaw and other apnea sufferers of that time had the availability of present-day diagnosis and access to continuous positive airway pressure (CPAP) treatment, they likely could have productively lived more years.

My cousin, Gloria, married in January 1959. She then moved to Mobile, where her military husband, Merton Middleton, was stationed. The month of February brought Mobile's anticipated celebration of Mardi Gras. Mobile's event was not touted as being as illustrious as New Orleans's famed brouhaha; nevertheless, an invitation from the newlyweds to visit them for the parades and festivities was super exciting for a sixteen-year-old country girl. The evening prior to my bus trip to Mobile, my generous Pawpaw pressed a ten-dollar bill, which was a significant amount, into my hand and urged me to enjoy myself. Pawpaw died unexpectedly a week later.

At Pawpaw's funeral, the Robinsonville Baptist Church was packed. Sheila, Pepper, and Janie, three of my eleventh-grade class-mates, sang his favorite hymn, "Rock of Ages." Pawpaw had an impressive bass voice. He, Mammaw, and I had often ridden the short distance across the Florida state line to Davisville School to enjoy Southern gospel music. Pawpaw especially enjoyed participat-ing in the sing-alongs. As friends and family gathered for his graveside service, I stayed close with my cousins, his seven other grandchildren. Soon the funeral director tugged me on the arm and ushered me to an empty chair reserved for Pawpaw's children. Taking the empty seat along with Dad and his three brothers affirmed that this was where I belonged. Pawpaw had indeed more than fulfilled a father's role for me, and I was, without a doubt, his little girl. During the funeral service, my classmate, friend, and neighbor, Douglas Owens, had volunteered to remain at our home to be a presence in the empty house. Some were concerned that, alerted by obituaries and news around the community that family and neighbors would likely be attending the funeral, our house left unattended could be vulnerable to potential burglars.

Doug, his brother, Roger, and their parents had joined many other neighbors at the wake the evening before. Wakes, also called visitation, were almost always held at the home of the departed. Immediate family received neighbors and friends who, in addition to their tearful condolences, brought enough food to literally feed the community. The casket containing the body of the deceased occu-pied a prominent place for viewing in the family's living room. I had withdrawn from the chatter to the quietness of my room to sob and to quietly contemplate what my life and Mammaw's would now be like without my beloved Pawpaw. At some point, there was a gentle tapping on my door. When I opened it, there was Doug holding a plate of food. "I thought you might be hungry," he said as he placed the plate in my hands. When he walked away, there was a sudden awareness that this childhood friendship was possibly…probably… moving to another level.

For the next few weeks, our close-knit family and community bonded even more tightly to help us process our grief and transition to life without our esteemed patriarch. Doug checked on us frequently to see how we were coping.

High School Days and a Budding Romance

As prom time approached for our eleventh-grade class, an attractive school friend, aware of my then-platonic friendship with Doug, asked me if he had a date for the upcoming prom. I did not know, but I assured her that I would ask him. If he did not, she asked if I would tell him that she would like to go with him. When I saw Doug walking near my locker a few days later, I called him over, saying that I needed to talk to him. He responded that he also needed to talk to me and then inquired about my need to talk to him. *This was a significant milestone when my response of "You go first..." forever changed my life.* Doug then shyly asked me to be his prom date. Without hesitation, I said yes. When Doug then asked what I needed to discuss with him, I shrugged and replied, "It's okay. Never mind." A couple of days later, when I explained to my forever friend, "So this is how it happened..." She giggled and wished us well. And she still does to this day.

When I was a young teenager, our polio vaccine was serum dropped on a sugar cube and taken orally over three scheduled doses. During the 1952 polio epidemic, over 3,000 people died, and more than 21,000 were permanently afflicted. The welcomed vaccine developed by American virologist and medical researcher Dr. Jonas Salk was made available in 1955. I had swallowed two of my three doses when I was scheduled for a tonsillectomy at Greenlawn Hospital in Atmore. When I showed up for surgery, the doctor learned that I had not completed the series of vaccines, and I was turned away.

Now in my late seventies, I still have my tonsils. An interesting fac-toid: the late Robert Sherman was frustrated. He had been hired to write appropriate lyrics for the upcoming Walt Disney *Mary Poppins* production. He had exhausted all ideas. In 1962, in response to his five-year-old son, Jeffrey's, explanation to his dad about how his polio vaccine had been easily administered orally that day, Robert was inspired to convert the method into music. As we know, the rest is history: "A Spoonful of Sugar Helps the Medicine Go Down."

I stepped up my resolve to overcome tonsillitis when Daddy discouraged my campaigning among Escambia County High School (ECHS) students to be elected cheerleader for the ECHS Blue Devils football and basketball teams. Dad was concerned that, with my his-tory of sore throat, I would be unable to fulfill my responsibilities with the cheerleading team. I campaigned. I won. I cheered. My sore throat was healed!

As a sponsored incentive for our small town's high school athletic program, Atmore's local Strand movie-theater management offered a complimentary movie every Thursday night during football season. Players and cheerleaders were given free admission, but everyone was required to purchase tickets for his or her date if the compan-ion was not in some way connected to the athletic program. As one might guess, neither Doug, who played football, nor I, a cheerleader, wanted to purchase an additional ticket. So with our complimentary passes, we went as a couple and sat together during the movies.

I looked forward to my involvement in school clubs and events. For me, like for many other classmates, it was easy to overload on extracurricular projects. The school counselors recognized that this could result in sacrificing one's academic focus. So in early spring, the administration developed a point system based on how much time was likely consumed by ancillary participation. In my senior year, in addition to classes, I was involved in about three clubs, including Beta Club. I was editor in chief of our school's award-winning news-paper, volunteering in the principal's office, and I was on the cheer-leading squad. When I received notice in late March that I would need to drop at least one activity to comply with the new point system, I gave up cheerleading. Football and basketball seasons were over. I had nothing to lose.

Miss Mary Hodnette, Escambia County High School's iconic English teacher who had also taught the generation before us, had never married. She called me aside one day to express her concern that my English grades were slipping from my typical honor-roll status. She wisely resorted to her years of experience and strategies when she suggested that she suspected that I was concentrating more on my relationship with Doug than on my English assignments. I was somewhat annoyed that she, a spinster, had the nerve to imply such a thing. Just to show her, I accelerated my study time to achieve that grade-A expectation.

After high school graduation in 1960, friends and family wondered if our commitment would survive Doug's four years at Troy State College, a three-hour drive away. When our high school staff and administrators showcased the annual College Recruitment Day, representatives from several southern colleges came to entice and recruit promising high school seniors. I was interviewed and, within a short time, offered a full scholarship in journalism to the University of Alabama. My college plans, as well as temporarily my relationship with my dad, were crushed when he refused to allow me to accept the award. I was graduating in the top 10 percent of my high school class, had excellent grades in English, and was editor in chief of *THE ESCOHI,* our high school newspaper. *THE ESCOHI* had ranked tops for our school's division in the state by Quill and Scroll, an international high school honor society that promoted excellence in journalism. However, Dad felt that the simmering dissension on college campuses in the 1960s was fertile ground for recruiting activists. The uprisings did gradually evolve into the hippie countercultural movement of the late 1960s and seventies. My family thought that if his authoritarian presumption had not been so harsh, it was almost humorous that Daddy used the excuse that I, always the peacemaker and compliant one, might become involved in some kind of uprising. Pleas from my principal, journalism teacher, and Mammaw to celebrate this achievement for me would not melt his hard heart.

Remaining obedient but with great despair, I witnessed the gift of a scholarship slip from my hands.

Doug was my rock as we together embraced the devastation of my dashed passion for becoming a journalist. We married at age nineteen when Doug was a college sophomore. We committed to each other that together we would overcome the pain of my being denied my dream degree. And we did indeed! That disappointment and others amazingly turned into blessings as I now look at most of my life in the rearview mirror. "Many are the plans in a person's heart, but it is the Lord's purpose that prevails" (Proverbs 19:21, NIV).

Our public grade schools were segregated. The black students attended Escambia County Training School in the segregated community known as "the quarters." Students from the Poarch Creek Indian Reservation joined us in junior high after attending the Poarch Consolidated School on the reservation from first through sixth grades. The teachers at Escambia County High School were not only sound educators, but they also pushed and challenged Doug and me and all their students to reach our full potential. One sad exception that haunts my memory took place in my ninth-grade science class. Our teacher was one of the football coaches, popular with the students because he was young, cute, flirtatious, and apparently more interested in being a classroom buddy than an instructor. Monday's class time during football season was usually spent recapping the highlights of Friday night's game.

Escambia County had pockets of extreme poverty. Several classmates came from these pockets. They were included as part of our class; however, they were excluded from bonding through extracurricular activities largely due to their responsibilities to help with family at home, on the farm, or at after-school jobs. John and McArthur were in my above-referenced science class. It was not hard to recognize McArthur's poverty disclosed by his ragged and faded jacket, which I vaguely remember was held together at the front by a safety pin. McArthur unintentionally created some minor disturbance causing our teacher/coach to call him to the front of the classroom for what I would wager was this gentle and sweet classmate's first-ever classroom disciplinary "offense." As small-framed McArthur fidgeted with the clasp to remove his jacket to take the powerful swings from Coach's reputable paddle, there was a corporate groan in the classroom. Breaking the silence came the nervous voice of John, tall and thin but not a stranger to trouble, "Let me take it for him, Coach." Seeming somewhat hesitant, Coach paused to process the awkward moment of perhaps having his authority challenged by John's benevolent offer.

Coach grasped the paddle and shouted to John, "Get up here!"

The paddling of John is one of the most daunting of my high school memories. Sadly, none in our class felt that we had an advocate to whom we could report the unacceptable behavior of this popular coach.

"No" Means *No*

Because my high school teachers, administrators, and classmates had respect for and confidence in me, I was entrusted with volunteer duties in the principal's office during my daily study period. Juggling schedule changes, office visitors, and unexpected opportunities kept me eagerly anticipating what each day might have in store.

One of those unexpected opportunities came when Mr. Robert R. Long, owner of Atmore's Ford dealership, visited the office to get a recommendation for an accountant from the principal, Mr. Travis Black. Mr. Black turned to my desk and said, "Hey, Faye, would you like to work for Mr. Long?" At age seventeen, still reeling from the loss of a scholarship and with graduation day approaching, I immediately accepted the job. I learned much about accounting and teamwork from my thirty-six-year-old coworker, Eulean (Chise) Davis, in my assigned responsibilities as accounts payable and accounts receivable clerk using a state-of-the-art Burroughs accounting machine. Employees were paid weekly in cash. In my additional duties as payroll clerk, on Saturdays, I collected time cards and figured the hourly wages for twenty-six employees. When I had calculated the total units for the denomination of bills and coins needed for each employee's respective pay envelope, I walked two blocks to First National Bank, cashed a company check, and returned with a money bag containing the weekly payroll. I hand-delivered each employee's pay envelope to his or her workstation before noon, Saturday's closing time. My two years of employment at Long Motor Company was an invaluable training experience that launched me into a lifetime accounting career.

However, there was a challenging chapter. Mammaw had wisely had "the talk" with me years earlier that coincided with the purchase of my first bra. In that conversation, she explained that God had wonderfully and amazingly designed our bodies. Until that moment, I had never given much thought to how I would change from a child into one who could conceive and bear a child. As she gave me a reassuring hug, she said that somewhere in our wide and wonderful world, God was at that moment changing the body of a boy into the man who would complement my physical, spiritual, and emotional needs as my lifetime partner. I wondered who he might be, how will we ever find each other, and how will I know that *he* is the one? God must have smiled as I pondered these thoughts. My lifelong companion would be Doug: my playmate, classmate, teammate, and soul mate. Although our love story did not have quite the enchantment of Cinderella's finding her prince, our story has achieved its fairytale ending "and they lived happily ever after."

During that talk, Mammaw clearly communicated that I was in complete charge of my body. Anyone touching or otherwise crossing my predetermined defined boundaries should firmly be told to stop. If the unwanted advances persisted, the perpetrator could/would be charged with assault or possibly rape. When I was approached by one of the respected staff at the Ford dealership on behalf of his "friend" to ask me to pose for questionable pictures in the dressing room of the friend's department store, my apprehension immediately activated my gift of fear, and I firmly said *no*. A few days later, the "offer" was repeated, suggesting that this might be my opportunity to launch a career in modeling. Instinctively, I knew that this longtime family friend was crossing that predetermined boundary. I immediately confronted him with a threat to tell my parents and/or our boss, Mr. Long. At this point, I told my stepmother. She and my dad were friends with both offenders. Her response was "If your dad finds out, this will not end well for these men." I am grateful that at eighteen years of age and with a moderate desire for fame and money, I had the discernment and courage to boldly confront the offender and would not compromise my values nor my body no matter what. That encounter reinforced my determination to protect myself. The experience has motivated and inspired me to face head-on whatever or whoever has been a threat or a challenge to my values or safety. My grandmother's proactively instilling in me that "no" means *no* put me on guard and possibly protected me from becoming one of the "Me Too" casualties.

Perhaps the fashion-modeling enticement prompted me to ask myself, "What's next?" Processing the reality that since college was no longer an option on my short-term radar, for what type of career could I prepare myself? Beryl, my influential stepmom, was a successful hairdresser. For the most part, she enjoyed her work. Daddy approved of her career; perhaps then, it would be okay for me. Soon I had enrolled in cosmetology school sixty miles away in Mobile, had given notice to leave my job, and had arranged to live with Uncle Aubrey and Aunt Eunice within easy busing distance to the school. For weeks, I privately struggled with the uncertainty of my decision to study cosmetology.

Two weeks before classes began, Mr. Long, owner of the Ford dealership, stood at my desk and solemnly asked me if he could talk with me privately. Positioning myself in a posh leather chair in front of his tidy desk, I was concerned about the somber look on Mr. Long's usually pleasant face. "Faye," he jumped right in, "is being a hairdresser what you really want to do?" I was shocked that he asked if this was something that *I* wanted to do! He was treating me as though I were a real person. It was reassuring that he, along with Mammaw, gave validity to my decisions and pushed me to reach my potential. Now at eighteen years of age, I was receiving affirmation from a respected, influential adult encouraging me to express my opinion about an important lifetime decision.

Without hesitation and with disbelief, my mouth spoke the words, "No, sir. It's not."

His response was "Well then, let's disregard your resignation. You can remain at your job here until you and Doug process your future plans together. And by the way, there will be a pay raise in your envelope starting this week to help the two of you plan for what's next."

As I walked throughout the dealership, I was captivated by a beautiful 1959 red and white Ford Fairlane 500 that had recently been repossessed. I knew, even without asking the price, that I could not afford such a dream car. Occasionally over the next few days, I would walk to the used car lot just to admire it. One of the salesmen, observing my arm's-length interest, reported to Mr. Long that I visited the car lot regularly to see if the Fairlane was still there. Again, one of my father figures, Mr. Long, came to my desk and said, "I hear that you are a regular visitor to check on a car in the used car lot." Somewhat embarrassed, I confessed that the red and white Fairlane 500 was beautiful, but I knew it was above what I could afford at this stage of my career. Within days, the car was mine! I simply picked up the ongoing payments and paid whatever I felt I could afford from each week's pay envelope. Mr. Long was a mentor who recognized the potential of his employees and encouraged each one to set and achieve their goals. On a few occasions, the salesman who alerted Mr. Long that I was interested in the car would tease me, saying, "When you get that car paid for, that old boy (Doug) is going to ask you to marry him!"

The new car showing event was a highlight for the dealership every fall. The new Ford models for the year arrived by rail or truck convoy and were draped to hide the new designs. Curtains were drawn as the cars were strategically stationed throughout the showroom and covered again until the unveiling celebration. Invitations were sent to old and potential new customers, and announcements were placed in local newspapers and in businesses around town to promote the occasion. Tables were elegant with floral arrangements and refreshments. Chise and I wore formal dresses. The men, from Mr. Long to the mechanics who changed oil and rotated tires, dressed as professionally as they could afford. It was quite a gala affair.

The Challenges of Adulting

One day in 1961, while at work at the Ford dealership, I received a phone call from Mother. She and Johnny were stateside after having been stationed for ten years in England and Morocco. Mother wanted to make arrangements to see me. Now eighteen years old, I had not seen Mother in ten years. I had never seen Johnny except in pictures. I phoned Dad, who was at work at the cucumber shed, and asked him to meet me at the drugstore soda fountain. When he arrived, already suspicious that something was up, he did not receive the news well. I told him that I really wanted and needed to see Mother after all those years. In anger, he told me to make up my mind that very day before I came home. If I intended to follow through to see Mother, I was no longer welcome in his house and should immediately find myself another place to live. Then he stormed out. Needless to say, I was useless at work for the remainder of the workday. If I chose to see Mother, where would I go? I needed a place *tonight*. Of course, Mammaw's house was my home, but I did not want to set up a volatile situation between my dad and his mother. Without a doubt, I knew my dad's brother, Uncle Vernon, and his wife would let me stay with them. So I phoned, sobbing to Aunt Margaret and shared about my dilemma. She assured me that I would always have a home with them. After Pawpaw's death, Mammaw had given Uncle Vernon land on which to build a house adjacent to her house and behind Pawpaw's store.

Leaving work at five, I anxiously drove my newly financed Ford to Uncle Vernon and Aunt Margaret's. Shortly on the heels of my arrival, Uncle Vernon met Dad, who was yelling and beating at the door. Uncle Vernon firmly told his brother that he was not welcomed to enter his home in that state of anger. Daddy went back to his car parked between Mammaw's house and Uncle Vernon's. Mammaw soon entered Uncle Vernon's house to persuade me to come work things out with Dad. Mammaw feared that in Daddy's anger, he would suffer a heart attack. When I went outside, Dad's temper had cooled, and we drove separately (me in my Ford) to his house, where I was living to be convenient to my workplace.

My stepmom Beryl and I picked out clothes for my special meeting with Mother within the next day or two. On my day's reunion with Mother and Johnny, they drove three hours to Troy so that they could meet Doug. Then they returned me to Atmore. After all this on one day's agenda, Mother and Johnny continued another two hours' drive to Castleberry to stay a few days with Mother's parents for the first time in a decade.

I had arrived at Dad and Beryl's house one evening and had changed from my work clothes to help serve dinner. Dad answered the ringing phone, centrally located in the hall. Moments later, he stood at the kitchen door, announcing tersely that the call was for me. The tone of his voice alerted me that something was wrong. My first thoughts were "Is Mother back in town?" or "Has something happened to Doug in Troy?" On the other end of the call was a forty-something-year-old male executive-type from Ford Motor Company, Atlanta's regional headquarters. He had been in the office conference room for the past couple of days in planning meetings with three or four salesmen and Mr. Long. I remembered being introduced upon his initial arrival. Other than the casual "hello" or "good morning" greeting, there had been little or no further interaction until now. He asked if I would accompany him to dinner in Pensacola that evening. My head swirled. *What? Who? Why me? Is he crazy?* I gathered my senses and quickly and firmly told him *no.* Dazed, I shuffled back into the kitchen. As one can imagine, Beryl's, Ron's, and especially Daddy's eyes were glaring at me.

"Who was that?" Daddy demanded, again in a curt tone. As I stumbled through an explanation that I was still trying to figure out myself, once again, I sensed Daddy's mistrust of me. Someone at the dealership had obviously given the caller my last name and/or phone number. Otherwise, he could not have tracked me.

Sobbing, I later confided to my loving Mammaw. She again assured me of Daddy's love for me. She bared her soul as she shared that Daddy feared I would follow Mother's reputation with men. How could Daddy, in his wildest imagination, think that I would forsake the deep values instilled by my grandparents and my church? I had committed my life to Christ. I had committed my relationship to Doug. My lifestyle evidenced that. Furthermore, I adored my Mammaw (Pawpaw had died two years earlier). I would do *nothing* to hurt or to bring embarrassment to her. Occasionally, she would remind me that I bore the Robinson name, a name long respected and which had not been tarnished by crime or other misbehavior. I had already concluded that the impeccable reputation she painted of my ancestors and extended family was somewhat exaggerated, yet I tried to do my part to epitomize the reputation Mammaw had of the family that she had married into.

The compelling movie *Days of Wine and Roses*, starring Jack Lemmon and Lee Ann Remmick, was nominated in 1963 for four Oscars, including best actor and best actress. The film's theme music, composed by Henry Mancini with lyrics by Johnny Mercer, won an Academy Award. After seeing the powerful film, I stood outside the theater entrance with my head lifted upward. At that moment, I vowed to God and to myself that I would never taste an alcoholic beverage. As I write this story fifty-eight years later, I have remained true to that promise.

Doug carpooled to Atmore almost every weekend. I continued working at Long Motor Company and paying weekly as much as I could on the car while managing to stash away a little savings. It was exciting to see the balance owed dwindle down to zero! The salesman's prediction about Doug's timing of the marriage proposal was accurate!

In 1961, the new Interstate 65 was under construction near Atmore. The overworked trucks were regularly brought into the Ford service department for maintenance and repair. Likewise, a frequent visitor to the Ford dealership was Hugh Stuart, supervisor of the road construction for the approximate twenty-four-mile stretch between Atmore and Big Escambia Creek toward Evergreen. Mr. Stuart was a handsome fellow, brawny, and suntanned from his outdoor work. He wore a Tilley-like hat twenty years before Alex Tilley founded the Canadian hat company in 1980. I always noticed his ring that wrapped his finger like a snake with a diamond for the snake's eye when Mr. Stuart was signing checks at the counter where I received payment for repairs on the construction trucks. I overheard Mr. Stuart and another customer discussing that he was in need of construction workers for the summer. Thinking that this might be a job Doug would be interested in, I asked Mr. Stuart about the possibility. He told me that when Doug came home from college, if he was interested, tell him to drive, dressed in his work clothes, up the dirt bed of now I-65 to the construction-site hut. Doug was to find Mr. Stuart to get his job assignment. And that's what Doug did. His main responsibility was refilling all the trucks at the fuel pump site. Additionally, Doug was to stand guard at the pumps to prevent local neighbors from using (stealing) the fuel to fill their private vehicles. The summer was hot, and the road construction was dirty, but the experience and the pay were good. Doug was able to afford an engagement ring for me later that year. I still wear and treasure that beautiful diamond, remembering the sacrifice he made so that I could have it.

Engagement, Marriage, and Starting Our Family

Following my extended family's traditional Thanksgiving dinner at Dad and Beryl's home, Doug followed Daddy into the backyard. There, like a just-turned nineteen-year-old true gentleman, Doug bravely told Daddy that he wanted to marry me. Daddy, as any dad would, asked how we planned to pay our bills. Between the two of us, Doug and I had saved $300 that was about one month's salary in 1962. My Christmas gift was the diamond engagement ring. We planned a June wedding and proceeded with plans for our marriage. In addition to verbal invitations to family, friends, and neighbors, our wedding invitation was published in *The Atmore Advance*, our local paper, with no RSVPs required. If I planned to invite Mother, then living in Shreveport, or any of my Kirkland relatives, Daddy threatened that he would boycott everything to do with the wedding, including any monetary contribution.

Our simple but beautiful Sunday afternoon ceremony was held at the First Baptist Church in Atmore with Doug's Troy State campus minister, Don Crapps, soloist, and Doug's college roommate, Clarence (Rusty) Ballard, a minister from Andalusia, officiating. Our high school classmate, Albert Kennington, a gifted organist, played as two teenagers in love beamed as Daddy (not beaming) and I walked down the aisle. I was wearing my beautiful wedding dress designed and sewn by my stepmother.

Faye and Doug's wedding

Doug's three groomsmen and my three attendants joined in the celebration of our union. The wedding ceremony was sandwiched between the morning and evening church services. This included the time for placement and removal of flowers, candles, and other basic decorations. We had no idea how many would attend the wedding nor the beautifully presented reception at Dad and Beryl's home. Beryl, family, and close friends provided ample refreshments for the houseful of reception guests. Another component that was in abundance was love between the two childhood playmates, sweethearts, and now husband and wife committed to have, hold, and cherish for the remainder of their lives.

En route to our honeymoon destination 50 miles away in Pensacola, Doug realized that he did not have our marriage license, which he was supposed to have gotten from the officiating minister. Being teenagers, and in the culture of the day, we feared that the motel would not rent us our reserved room without proof of marriage. We returned to Atmore, hoping, but doubtful, that we would find Clarence before his departure to Troy. Doug, knowing his roommate well, found him still in Atmore at the local hangout, McMurphy's Dairy Bar. Soon, legally documented, we proceeded to Pensacola for dinner at the Holiday Inn and to our affordable honeymoon suite.

Both our families made it clear that they were unable to help us financially. However, during our early years of marriage and babies, Doug's parents provided endless produce and meats from their farm. My stepmother, Beryl, lovingly sewed dresses for me and later for our two daughters.

One week following our wedding, Doug began his junior year at Troy State College (TSC), and I began my exciting position as secretary to the Troy State Physical Education Department. I joined with Doug at Calvary Baptist Church, where he continued his employment as a part-time music director. We walked the aisle together on our first Sunday at church as husband and wife and publicly dedicated our home, wherever and whatever, to honor Christ: a commitment that has remained a priority and a blessing throughout our marriage.

Working as secretary to athletic director Dr. Earl Grant Watson at TSC was yet another significant step toward preparing me for future career opportunities. I looked forward to every day's responsibilities and adventures while being an administrative assistant to all the Troy State coaching staff and faculty. Fondly referred to as "pack rats" by Dr. Watson and known throughout the TSC campus as pack rats, six male students were granted student assistantships and, when not in their classes, were available to do various chores for the department faculty, maintain the football fields, and other responsibilities related to the upkeep of the athletic facilities.

To supplement our income, Doug mowed Doc Watson's lawn while the Watson family enjoyed a month's vacation during the summers of 1962 and 1963. My responsibility was to feed and care for the Watson family pets while Doug cut the grass. Dr. Watson was particular about the way his grass was to be meticulously cut twice weekly, at an exact height, diagonally northwest to southeast for the first cutting of the week and southwest to northeast on the second cutting. Since that lesson in mowing, Doug has insisted that our lawn is cut using Doc Watson's mowing method.

Another supplement to our income came from my working for an elderly writer living in Troy. She hired me to type with carbon copy, mind you, her handwritten manuscripts for submission to

Reader's Digest. Several of her stories were successfully published in the popular magazine. She seldom spent time visiting, but she always provided freshly baked cookies and milk as I sat typing for an hour or two following my eight-hour day's work in the Physical Education Department. My work area was her neat, small porch, ventilated by the trendy 1960s jalousie glass windows that conveniently tilted to pull a breeze to cool my body pregnant with our first child. When I left work, she always handed me my pay in cash, along with a brown bag containing the remaining cookies.

In October 1962, four months after our marriage, the Cold War confrontation known as the Cuban Missile Crisis between the United States and the Soviet Union was not only a national crisis but also brought family alarm when Doug was notified that his selective-service draft status had moved to 1-A, the next to be drafted. The two superpowers came close to nuclear conflict initiated by the American discovery of Soviet ballistic-missile capability in Cuba, only 90 miles off the coast of Florida. After days of fear, tears, and prayer, Doug's draft status was reassigned to a lower status because he was both married and a full-time student.

Grateful for the reprieve, we moved on with life. Doug worked as a janitor at Troy State's Baptist Student Center. We bought a two-bedroom trailer in Troy State's married students' trailer park, where we lived happily for Doug's remaining eighteen months as a student. It was in that trailer where we entertained our friends as though we lived in a mansion. It was in that home sixteen months later that we welcomed our first precious baby daughter, Debra Lynn.

I thought it was significant that we received the positive pregnancy report on Valentine's Day. Not knowing if our baby was a girl or boy until her birth, baby-shower gifts, plus the few necessities we purchased, were generic. We were too naive to be anxious about birthing our first child. Doug and I went about life and work pretty much as usual. Interestingly, so routinely that Doug *forgot* that an important book review coincided with our baby's due date. His memory was jogged when my labor pains began. In response to Doug's call to Dr. Jesse Hall Colley, the doctor recommended that we should make our way to the hospital. Doug inquired of the doctor if he thought I might have time to type his report. I am not aware of Dr. Colley's reply but, taking the risk, out came the portable typewriter and the partially handwritten report. While I typed, Doug wrote. By midnight, the report was complete, and my labor pains were more frequent and more intense.

We arrived at Beard Memorial Hospital in plenty of time for Debbie's arrival near eight o'clock the next morning. When I was wheeled from the delivery room, Doug asked how I was feeling. He thought that it was strange when I replied that my head was exploding. Even with my pounding headache, both of us chuckled when Doug replied, "Your head?" Within the next few minutes, the medical team scrambled to get my rising blood pressure under control. Concerned that seeing my newborn could cause an adverse effect on my elevated blood pressure, my doctor's decision was that it would be better if I did not see the baby until my blood pressure stabilized to a more normal level. That did not happen until the following day because I lay wondering and worrying about what was wrong with my baby to prompt the medical team's decision that it was best that I did not see her. In my twilight zone from medication, I conjured up the reason was that my baby did not have an arm. During my early pregnancy, when I experienced minor morning sickness, I determined that I would never consider taking the common morning sickness medication, thalidomide. Thankfully, during both my pregnancies, I experienced only minor discomforts and endured those without seeking relief from any prescribed or over-the-counter medications, including aspirin. It was confirmed too late for many babies born worldwide with severe abnormal development, some with deformed extremities, that thalidomide taken by their unsuspecting pregnant mothers had apparently caused their crippling afflictions. The best cure for my blood pressure a day later was to see and hold our beautiful, healthy, seven-pound thirteen-ounce bundle who had all her extremities and a great pair of lungs.

Doug's First Teaching Job and Our Move to Georgia

After our marriage, Doug accelerated his class load to include two summer terms and earned his bachelor's degree from Troy State in November 1963. He was student-teaching at Goshen High School near Troy that fateful day when President Kennedy was assassinated. Our anxieties about Doug's finding a high school math teacher position two months into the school year were temporary when he learned of and applied for three positions in middle Georgia. With five-week-old baby Debbie in tow, our young family of three drove to Vienna (Dooley County), Cordele (Crisp County), and Montezuma (Macon County) for scheduled interviews in early November. Doug was hired on the spot following the Macon County interview. His annual base salary was $3,750 plus a $500 bonus as a math teacher. The following 1964 school term, another $700 bonus was added for his football coaching assistance.

Excited about Doug's new job and our life's next chapter, we sold our trailer home in Troy for the same price we had paid for it eighteen months earlier and moved into a furnished duplex on Railroad Street in Montezuma. We rented from an elderly couple who lived in the other half of the house. To supplement their retirement income, the Arnolds had added the furnished apartment. Doug could easily walk across the street and railroad to Macon County High School. Having just turned twenty-one, Doug daily wore a tie to identify himself as a teacher to the students, one of whom was nineteen and repeating twelfth grade.

We were welcomed with true Southern hospitality into Montezuma's school, community, and church life. Within a few months, we learned that a church family was relocating due to a job transfer. We rented their two-bedroom home, which was located on a quiet street near the location where the new high school was under construction. I was emotionally torn at this same time with the decision between being a stay-at-home mom or satisfying my desire to get back into the workplace. I applied to Southern Frozen Foods Inc. and was hired as secretary to Mr. Hal Stewart, vice president in charge of sales. During the 1960s, Southern Frozen Foods was the largest producer of frozen vegetables in the country. Once again, this was the perfect job for me: working in an office with about ten women and half a dozen men. With the exception of two coworkers who continued their longevity of not speaking to each other, it was a happy, congenial workplace. The assembly lines for weighing, grading, freezing, and the packing process assured year-round employment for hundreds in the area. In no time, Doug and I felt we would plant our lives forever in this then-thriving small agricultural town in the heart of peach, peanut, and pecan country.

One of Doug's students was Dovie Hutto, who lived nearby with her widowed mother, Carolyn. Dovie became our regular babysitter. Typically, it was more convenient for us to leave baby Debbie at the Hutto home, nurturing a forever bond between Dovie, Carolyn, and Debbie. This dear mother-and-daughter team was a godsend, not only for lovingly caring for our babies, but also for emotionally adopting all four of us as a family until their deaths four months apart in 2019 and 2020, when Carolyn was in her nineties, and Dovie was in her seventies.

Doug was resolute to have a positive influence beyond the classroom in the lives of his students. He made himself available to tutor his students after school. He was earning a pay bonus for time spent as assistant football coach for the junior high school team. Debbie, now a toddler, and I enjoyed traveling during football season with Doug when he scouted (spied on) football plays and strategies of out-of-town teams scheduled for later competition with Macon County's varsity Rebels. Doug spent Saturday nights supervising activities at the newly organized Macon County Youth Center. Meanwhile, I began to become somewhat discontented with my home-work-home-work routine.

Georgia Southwestern College was located twenty miles away in Americus. The proximity of an educational institution nearby awakened a hibernating dream. My employers at Southern Frozen Foods encouraged me to seize the opportunity. They cooperated in arranging my work responsibilities around my class schedule. Debbie was being well cared for during the day by Lillie Bell Solomon, a dear black woman, who not only doted on Debbie and cleaned our small home but also had food prepared so I could eat lunch, love on Debbie, and get back to work in due time.

Even with everything seemingly in place to continue my education, there was just not enough of me left after working half a day, driving an hour roundtrip to Americus to attend class, and then home to study. My inherent temperament to excel in all my roles began to take its toll. When two-year-old Debbie crawled into my lap one night, interrupting my homework and snuggling into my arms, I realized that any other person could fill my position as an employee, student, Sunday school teacher, or any other role, but only I could be Deb's mom. Shortly after my withdrawal from Georgia Southwestern classes and realizing, with no regrets, that my role as mom superseded all other responsibilities, I learned that I was pregnant with our second child.

During my 1966 summer of pregnancy, I continued my job at Southern Frozen Foods, and Doug spent the summer of 1966 on-site at Auburn University. He lived in a dormitory Sunday through Thursday nights and returned to Montezuma for the weekends. I was an impressive pitcher for Cedar Valley Baptist Church's softball team in the local women's league. Cute Debbie, with her congenial personality, looked forward to the attention she received from Cedar Valley's church members who came to the softball field. She always sought out Roy and Helen Jones because Roy fed her fresh roasted peanuts while cheering for the Cedar Valley team. I resigned from my team position in my fourth month of pregnancy.

Four days after our baby's due date had passed, Dr. A. J. Morris tried unsuccessfully to persuade me to allow him to induce labor. He jokingly said that he would not come if I went into labor and interrupted his night's sleep. That very night when I arrived in labor at Montezuma's Riverside Hospital, there were two nurses on duty. I knew I was in trouble when the practical nurse who was prepping me for delivery observed the stretch marks on my abdomen from my previous pregnancy and asked me if those were scars from a hysterectomy. Later she announced to the registered nurse (RN) in the delivery room that because she had a headache, she did not feel up to assisting with delivering a baby. She went home later, leaving my well-being and that of my unborn child in the hands of the RN and Doug. Fathers-to-be were banished from the delivery room in those days for fear they might require medical attention themselves and distract or otherwise interfere with the medical team. Not so for this birth! Doug opened the private entrance door to the delivery room when Dr. Morris arrived just in time to cut the umbilical cord and to announce the birth of our second daughter, Sharilyn. It was after the baby's arrival that I received my first medication, including any painkiller. Looking through the hospital nursery window the following day, I was alarmed that my baby's crib was empty. Upon returning to my room, I found a nurse walking into other patients' rooms to show off the new baby in town…and allowing them to cuddle the newborn. She survived!

In February of 1967, we moved to a rental house located in a pecan orchard and with a sizable garden plot that appealed to us. A pony belonging to our landlord grazed in the orchard and was available for Debbie to ride when the owner was present. One day, Doug and I worked nearby in our garden while baby Sharilyn sat in her stroller, entertained by her four-year-old sister, who was playing on the sliding board. When the interactive baby chatter and laughter ceased, I instinctively did a quick mommy-check. Debbie, pretending that she was a pony, had looped a rope around her neck and tied the other end to the top of the slide. Debbie was choking about halfway down the slide. In a flash, I arrived on the scene to rescue her. Another miracle!

In the fall of that year, with the emotional longing and the financial need to return to work, I was hired as school secretary at Macon County High School, where Doug was beginning his fifth year as a math teacher. As with every working parent, we faced the difficult chore of finding a responsible person who would be a loving caregiver for our two little girls. With no screening reviews like those provided by today's online searches, we learned of a possible candidate who had previously worked for a prominent family in town. Doug and I, along with Debbie, almost four, and Sharilyn, almost one, met with her. With some reservations, we hired her for childcare and light housekeeping.

I left adequate food for our new caregiver and instructions for the lunch menu that I had prepared for Debbie and preselected toddler food for Sharilyn. One evening, I discovered a slice of stale loaf bread behind the TV. Debbie answered my inquiry by saying that she had been given the bread for her lunch. Debbie hid it because she didn't want plain bread. Meanwhile, the lunch in the fridge designated for Deb was gone. Finding childcare in small-town Montezuma was difficult at best, so I hoped that a reminder to our caregiver to feed the children their prepared lunches would be adequate.

A few days later, our mail carrier, whose wife worked with me at Macon County High School, stopped by the school after his midday mail delivery. He had gone to the door of our house that we rented from his brother to hand-deliver a package. Sensing that things did not seem quite right, he entered the house to check. His report to me about the physical condition of my children, especially my baby, was alarming. Sharilyn was apparently still in her crib, diaper not changed, and reaching for him to take her. I left for home immediately, paid the "caregiver," and drove her home. I phoned a church friend who had two children close in age to ours. Margaret, a stay-at-home mom, readily agreed to keep Debbie and Sharilyn for the remaining four weeks of the school year.

Sputnik's Impact

Russia's October 4, 1957, successful launch of beachball-sized 184-pound Sputnik 1 that could orbit the earth in ninety-eight minutes brought about another opportunity for us. News of the launch stunned the world and shifted dynamics in the United States to accelerate lagging space endeavors. Competition in the race for space exploration during the Cold War suddenly escalated to an urgent level of defense, education, and job training. The wave of national anxiety and crushed pride pressured Congress to pass the National Defense Education Act (NDEA) in 1958 and to boost the 1959 appropriation for the National Science Foundation (NSF) by almost an additional $100 million over the previous year. Doug's undergraduate program at Troy State had been financed with an NDEA loan. The loan was forgivable at 10 percent per year of full-time teaching up to 50 percent with five years of teaching service. The NSF now began pouring the additional funds into revolutionizing new curriculums and technologies to reform the teaching of mathematics and sciences. Sixty-one years later in 2018, President Trump commissioned the Pentagon to establish a sixth independent military service branch to undertake missions and operations in the rapidly evolving space domain. The U.S. Space Force is the first new military branch since the 1947 establishment of the U.S. Air Force.

Following Doug's evening courses during the 1965–1966 school year offered by Auburn University at nearby Georgia Southwestern College, he applied for and was awarded an NSF Summer Institute Grant to work toward his master's degree in mathematics education. While working on his master's paper, and in addition to his teaching duties at Macon County High School, Doug regularly drove the 140-mile roundtrip to his advisor's home in Columbus, Georgia, to get feedback, critique, and direction.

The following summer of 1967, when Doug returned to Auburn's campus for his second quarter again funded by the NSF grant, he and I, along with three-year-old Debbie, baby Sharilyn, and chihuahua Bama, lived in a rented three-bedroom trailer near campus and enjoyed the summer together as a family. We stayed in Auburn during the week and returned to Montezuma on weekends to harvest our vegetable crops and worship with our Cedar Valley Baptist Church friends.

On a weekend back in Montezuma during peach season, we headed out to pick peaches in one of the many surrounding orchards. While Doug turned the car around in our driveway with shirtless Sharilyn in her car seat and Debbie in the back seat, I dashed back into our house to get a top for Sharilyn. Returning to the car, I screamed when I saw Debbie open the back door and tumble underneath the moving car. She had asked Doug if she could open the door, and as he said no, Debbie had already pulled the handle, and the door flung open, dragging her with it. Frantically but cautiously, Doug reversed the car and backed the tire off the back of Debbie's knee. We remained relatively calm as we drove to the local hospital and were very thankful and relieved that the x-ray showed no major injury. In a couple of days, other than bruising, minor swelling, and soreness, Debbie was pretty much back into routine.

Doug completed his master of education degree at Auburn that summer of 1967. Upon his graduation, I was awarded my Putting Hubby Through (PHT) degree that I not only thought to be clever, but I also took its kudos to heart. The degree was awarded to the wives of graduates by the university president's wife, Pauline Philpott. Auburn University's first lady knew firsthand the investment and personal sacrifices contributed by the wife to the earning of the husband's degree. On that note, it is interesting that, sadly, there were no Putting Wives Through awards. As I reflect on that era, and even into this year 2021, there are few men who have sacrificed for their wives' graduate degrees. I applaud the resolve of my female friends who have earned their doctorates. Some have succeeded without the support of their husbands, and some saw their marriages dissolve when the husband failed to support his wife in pursuit of her career goals.

In 1968, Doug received the third summer of NSF Summer Institute funding from the University of Georgia (UGA) in Athens. At this juncture, and on the heels of the NSF Summer Institute grants, Doug received a fellowship from the mathematics education program at UGA funded by the U.S. Department of Education to provide financial support for his doctoral studies. UGA was chartered in 1785, giving the institution the distinction of being the oldest state-chartered institution in the country. We overcame the sadness of moving from our comfort zone in Montezuma, a sleepy little middle-Georgia farm town, to embrace the challenging unknown.

We moved to Athens in the spring of 1968 after Doug finished his teaching contract with Macon County. We temporarily moved into an adequate, though dark and damp, basement suite on Athens's east side. Doug began his graduate program, and our children and I transitioned into our next chapter. Shortly after our move, while I was watching over Debbie and Sharilyn as they played on their swing set that we had moved from Montezuma, two neighboring women, strangers at that time, stopped. They invited our four-year-old to their nearby church's upcoming Vacation Bible School (VBS). I agreed and also accepted their offer to transport her. Those two hospitable neighbors remain dear friends to this day, fifty-plus years later.

Numerous friendships resulted from Debbie's attending VBS. We joined Johnson Drive Baptist Church and remained members there for three years until we moved to Doug's position at the University of British Columbia (UBC) in 1971. The small Johnson Drive congregation embraced us with love and care. Church members, Luther and Sybil Gooch, were owners of poultry houses that produced thousands of chickens annually for Central Soya, a local slaughter and processing plant. Needless to say, Luther and Sybil kept our freezer supplied with fryers. My most amusing recollection was when Doug helped Luther one morning on the Gooch farm and returned home with a share of field peas that Doug and Luther had picked and divided. Sybil arrived on our porch that afternoon, where I was diligently shelling and meticulously picking through the wormy and bug-damaged produce. The peas were not only fresh vegetables for our family; more importantly, they were *free*. Sybil insisted that she was taking my remaining half-bushel home to help me shell them. She called a while later to confess that on her way home, she threw the unshelled, infested peas into a trash dumpster. Even now, when we are faced with a formidable task, Doug and I fondly remember her kind gesture of throwing out the bad peas. We often comment, "Where is Sybil when you need her?"

To help our daughters in transitioning to their new Athens home, Doug and I decided a wading pool would be ideal for them to splash in to cool themselves from the heat of the Georgia summer. After purchasing the molded plastic pool at K-Mart and getting it to the car, we realized that it would not fit into the trunk. This is one of those "you-would-have-had-to-be-there" moments. Surveying the situation and our few options to secure the pool, we tied long shoelaces together with the intention to make a grip for both driver and passenger to hold outside our opened windows, attached the shoelaces to the pool now upside down on top of the car, and began our five-mile adventurous delivery. Not far along the way, the wind, as we traveled, lifted the pool from our grasp and hurled it, thankfully, into a ditch rather than into the traffic. The children who, until this potential disaster, had calmly taken it all in as Mommy and Daddy were showing them how to haul a purchase too big for transporting inside the car. They began crying and accusing us of tearing up their pool. Finally, we reached home with the pool intact, but the family… not so much. When we moved the pool onto the grassy lawn and tore the paper label from the inside bottom, we read the unforgettable words, "Pool may be folded for easy transport."

Moving On and Moving Up

During our three-month occupancy of the basement suite, baby Sharilyn awoke one morning with a seriously swollen eyelid. Diagnosed by a quickly located doctor, Sharilyn was treated for a spider bite. At this point, we began to look for more suitable, yet affordable, living accommodations. Our next home was a rented duplex near the intersection of Milledge Avenue and West Broad Street. Athens neighborhoods were segregated in 1968. Ours was the last white-occupied house on Reese Street adjacent to the black neighborhood. We lived well in that home and clung to many cherished memories. Our backyard was private with a fence on the west separating us from a kind elderly couple, Mr. and Mrs. Smith, whose pecans we picked up, and they shared generously with us. The adjacent east property was significantly lower, requiring a retaining wall. The spacious backyard was ideal for our children's swing set and a small garden where we grew tomatoes. It provided a safe refuge for our chihuahua-mix, Bama, to hide after he had taunted the neighbor's German shepherd until the big dawg had enough. Another favorite adventure for Bama was his routine trek across the light traffic of Reese Street to Kentucky Fried Chicken, where patrons encouraged Bama's delinquency and pudginess by tossing him chicken scraps.

Doug's Department of Education grant paid his tuition plus a small stipend for living expenses, but this was not adequate to sustain the budget for a family of four. Again, faced with the tension between being a stay-at-home mom or providing for our family's basic financial needs, I became an Avon representative with an assigned client territory. I was quite successful and welcomed the flexibility of ringing doorbells when Doug could study at home and be with our children. I made new friends among my clientele, and I earned enough extra income to provide groceries plus some extras.

One of my customers connected me with Louise Thompson, American Cancer Society coordinator for seven north Georgia counties. Needing part-time office help, Ms. Thompson hired and trained me to schedule her fundraiser events and maintain accounts for donors' records of charitable giving throughout her region. Ms. Thompson allowed me total flexibility to be at home or to work on-site as demands required. To encourage me further, she bought Avon products each sales period to help me achieve my quota. When Doug accepted the position at the University of British Columbia, as a going-away remembrance, Ms. Thompson gave me a gold bracelet with an American Cancer Society charm engraved with the year 1971.

Doug's approaching November birthday in 1969 reminded me of the previous winter when he needed a lightweight, warm jacket, but other priorities drained any extra cash. The chief petty officer (CPO) jacket was popular. I thought that style would be ideal for Doug, so I began to stash away my Avon earnings while keeping my eyes on the local department stores' sales. When the perfect jacket appeared in the flyer, I excitedly and discreetly slipped away with my envelope of cash to purchase Doug's birthday gift. My heart sank when the clerk told me they were sold out of his size. She offered to order the jacket, and I agreed. Then came the phone call that the jacket had been back-ordered, and it would not arrive for a couple more weeks, barely in time for his birthday. By the time the order arrived, some more urgent need had exhausted the cash that I had saved. My neighbor loaned me the money to buy the jacket. Doug still occasionally wears the worn-out jacket around the house. I have the feeling that his wearing it still gives him a hug.

The reputable preschool and kindergarten programs were the draw that began our endearing relationship with Beech Haven Baptist Church. The teachers, Jane Eldridge and Jane McMullen, provided a sound preschool foundation for our daughters in a safe environment. Although the tuition was reasonable, it stretched our tight stipend income. I am forever grateful that my stepfather, John Bell, on his benevolent initiative, sent monthly checks to cover the tuition of preschool for Sharilyn and kindergarten for Debbie.

All Athens memories were not pleasant. In April 1970, African American high school students, frustrated over their loss of Burney Harris High School, began a month-long protest. Burney Harris was not only the one surviving black high school in Clarke County but, since 1868, the school had also played a significant role as the community center for African Americans. The Department of Health, Education, and Welfare was pressuring the Clarke County school board to desegregate the high schools. When Burney Harris and Athens High School students and parents became aware of the board's decision to no longer designate the school for black students, and without input from the African American community, the ensuing protests attracted national attention with news coverage within our neighborhood, specifically at the intersection of Milledge and West Broad Streets, one block from our duplex.

The second unsettling event was on Friday, July 17, 1970. Late in the evening, a tanker-truck driver was transferring gasoline to a storage tank at the Texaco compound on North Hull Street. The fumes were ignited by a pilot light close by, and the truck exploded, along with three of the five storage tanks, sending flames as high as 500 feet. The flames were reportedly seen as far as 15 miles away, and the blast could be heard for miles. According to the archived AP news article published in the *New York Times*, the explosion "left 715 persons homeless, 46 injured, and property damage estimated at $500,000 to $1,000,000." Debbie and Sharilyn had been fed, bathed, story told, prayers said, and were sleeping when the explosion rocked our duplex, rattling windows and dishes. The wall clock began chiming at an off-hour response to the boom. Doug was studying at the university. With the strength of a frightened mom, I dragged the two beds, with our sleeping children, from the rattling windows in case there should be a second blast. I rushed to the front door in response to panic in the streets and watched frightened and helplessly as people, some in their pajamas, ran screaming while the night sky rolled red. My first thought was "This is the rapture, and these poor people were left behind." Then came the sobering jolt. "Oh, no! I was left behind too!"

When Doug's dissertation topic had been identified, research completed, and compilation begun, I began the nightly endeavor of typing his paper. Data input for the 255-page document with two carbon copies was managed on a rented state-of-the-art technology of the day, an Underwood electric typewriter. Two invisible erasures per page were allowed. The required top, bottom, right, and left margins were defined by measuring with a ruler and lightly marked with a pencil. Doug and I typically got to bed late each night after this arduous process. The following day, Doug's professor, Dr. Les Steffe, would review and make corrections. Any minor change required retyping, original with two carbons, from the point of any correction forward to the end of the respective chapter. I have a great appreciation for today's technology with autocorrect, cut, paste, and delete capability.

Opportunity in Canada, Eh?

Although we knew our time in Athens was likely limited to Doug's completion of his degree, we could not keep our emotions from becoming deeply rooted in the amiable culture. In April 1971, Doug attended the National Council of Teachers of Mathematics (NCTM) in Anaheim, California. During a daily call to check on his family and to update his news from the conference, Doug chuckled as he told me that he had scheduled an unexpected interview with a search committee from the University of British Columbia (UBC) located in Vancouver. Neither of us took the interview too seriously. The committee asked Doug to send his resumé to UBC, which he agreed to do when he returned to Georgia. Arriving home and somewhat hesitant about moving his family to another country, Doug quickly immersed himself into wrapping up his dissertation and coursework to complete his degree at UGA. About two weeks later, and not having received the promised resumé, the associate dean phoned Doug to inquire, and to which Doug responded, "I will have it in tomorrow's mail." The rest is history. We departed in August 1971 on the nearly three-thousand-mile journey with all appropriate documentation to enter Canada. We told family and friends that we would return in 1973 after fulfilling Doug's two-year contract. Little did we know that God was smiling because He, once again, had different plans. "'For I know the plans I have for you,' declares the Lord, 'plans to prosper you and not to harm you, plans to give you hope and a future'" (Jeremiah 29:11, NIV).

A few weeks prior to our August 13 departure from Athens, a university friend, who was aware of our imminent move to

Vancouver, put us in contact with Beryl Butterfield. Beryl, who lived in the greater Vancouver area (population approximately 2.5 million), was researching her Butterfield genealogy at the University of Georgia. Beryl's ancestor, John Butterfield, was the owner of the historic Butterfield Stage Lines, which partnered in the mid-1800s with Wells Fargo & Company Stage Lines. Two weeks before Beryl's return to Vancouver, she eagerly accepted our invitation to dinner. She spent the evening orienting us to her city and graciously offered to assist us in preparation for our arrival. Before leaving our home, Beryl asked our children if they had questions about moving to their new country. Upon inquiring, four-year-old Sharilyn was ready to move with the assurance that her favorite TV show, *Heehaw*, would indeed be available.

The University of British Columbia reimbursed our moving expenses from Athens to Vancouver. All personal belongings had to be documented in a general category, along with individual medical records for each of us, to present to Canada's immigration officials upon arrival at the international border. In addition to the moving van, we loaded a trailer that Doug had rigged. In reality, it was not a trailer but the bed of an old pickup truck that Doug had purchased nine years earlier from a junk dealer in Atmore. Planning ahead for moving our scarce belongings from Atmore to Troy following our wedding, Doug, with the help of a welder, converted the steel pickup bed into a trailer to hitch behind our car. We were clones of the *Beverly Hillbillies* as we drove approximately three thousand miles to Vancouver, stopping in Atmore and Shreveport to bid tearful farewells to our families, who would not see their granddaughters nor us for another eighteen months.

Doug and I made every effort to make the trip exciting for our daughters, ages four and seven. We made a big deal about crossing the Mississippi River and visiting historic venues. After the service at our impromptu visit to Oklahoma City's First Baptist Church, someone tapped Doug on the shoulder, mistaking him to be Doug's brother, Roger. Who would have ever dreamed that in that mega congregation, we would see someone we knew? Arthur Mack had not only grown up in Atmore but also specifically in our small community of

Martinville. Realizing who we were, he immediately insisted that we join him and his pregnant wife at their home for dinner. Reluctantly, because there was no way to alert her, we four extra bodies showed up at their home for Sunday dinner. She graciously welcomed us, and we enjoyed the meal, hospitality, and an unexpected reunion.

Another milestone along the trip was the breathtaking scene unfolding as we approached the Grand Tetons on the western horizon. I burst into tears, not only overwhelmed by the majestic view but also at the sudden realization that I was so far from home. In 2018 when our daughter Debra rode with us from Georgia to British Columbia and returned, the three of us again experienced that imposing spectacle. Remarkably, Debra remembered the spot where forty-seven years earlier, she first saw the snowcapped peaks seeming to pierce the azure sky. The adult Debra would not relent until she found the exact spot and, once again, stood in awe where she recaptured and refreshed that enduring memory. Only the ripples from the school of trout competing for the dragonfly alighted on the reeds interfered with the mountains' reflection in the crystal clear lake.

Continuing to Salt Lake City on our 1971 move, we toured the Visitors Center at the Mormon Tabernacle and experienced what and where non-Mormon visitors were allowed. Seeing the Great Salt Lake was an awesome fulfillment of one of my childhood dreams. Floating together as a family on the vast buoyant and salt-laden lake was a fun experience for all except four-year-old Sharilyn, whose freshly scratched mosquito bites, which she had incurred along the road trip, reacted painfully to the briny water. A few tears later and after hosing off with fresh water that was provided for the adventurous guests who risked a dip in the lake, Sharilyn, at last, experienced relief from the stinging salt. The purchase of souvenir brine shrimp, which the gift shop cleverly marketed to children as "sea monkeys," brought giggles and contributed to their lifelong memories. The Petrified Forest in Washington state was another iconic memory on August 26, 1971, as we adults emotionally prepared for our family's entry into Canada the following day.

Finally, the day arrived, *August 27, 1971, another day providentially placed in our odyssey that historically would change the courses of our lives—all four of us—forever!*

The impressive Peace Arch, a sixty-seven-foot monument, was a welcomed sight at the end of our long, adventurous journey. The concrete structure's construction began in July 1920 to mark 100 years of peace resulting from treaties between the United States and Great Britain at the end of the War of 1812. The flags of the United States and Canada are mounted on the crown of the arch. The inscription on the U.S. side of the frieze reads, "Children of a common mother," and the words on the Canadian side read, "Brethren dwelling together in unity." Within the arch, each side has an iron gate mounted on both sides of the border with an inscription above each gate. On the east side, the inscription reads, "May these gates never be closed." To commemorate the centennial of the friendship between the two nations, the inscription on the west side reads, "1814 Open One Hundred Years 1914."

Welcome to Canada

We waited somewhat anxiously as Canadian immigration officers meticulously combed through our thoroughly prepared and organized entry documents, including the "Goods to Follow," an itemized list of all that was to arrive at the border within a few days on the moving van. Finally, we were relieved that we would be admitted to Canada as documented "landed immigrants," and we found the way to our new home. Friends, who had immigrated previously, had alerted us that we would likely find Canadians somewhat reserved compared to Americans in general and to Georgians (Southerners) in particular. One American couple, who had immigrated earlier, told us not to expect neighbors to bring cookies or have much to do with us for a while until they decided whether they liked us. With this in mind and assuring myself that they *would* like us if they gave us a chance, we arrived at the duplex that Beryl, the Canadian we had met in Georgia, had found for us. The apartment was about 10 kilometers (6.2 miles) from the university and walking distance (albeit across a busy intersection with a traffic light) to the school where Debbie and Sharilyn would attend. Beryl had presented the vaccinations certificates and all the other required information that we had given her in Georgia to successfully enroll Sharilyn in kindergarten and Debbie in grade three (yes, *not* third grade) at General Gordon Elementary School. We were all set!

We three girls were excited that our duplex was four blocks from Kitsilano Beach on English Bay. Even in August, we found the water too cold for swimming. Until acclimated, I sat bundled in my beach towel, observing other swimmers behaving as though they were on the balmy beaches of the Gulf of Mexico, for which I was beginning to long. To be totally transparent, for the twenty-one years we lived in the Vancouver area, I never enjoyed swimming in the cold water. I soon learned that the area had so much more to offer to compensate, such as mountains, ranches, boating, lovely gardens, and a variety of events that eventually became our family traditions. Favorites were the Cloverdale Rodeo on Victoria Day (a celebration of Queen Victoria's birthday on the last Monday in May preceding May 25) and kicked off by a free pancake breakfast at Guildford Mall, and the thrilling Abbotsford Air Show in August. The anticipated annual Pacific National Exhibition (PNE) seventeen-day summer fair with its seasonal amusement park and arena ran from mid-August through Labour Day and was a melting pot of fun and entertainment, transcending any and all cultural barriers.

We looked forward to Canada Day celebrations on July 1, marking the anniversary of the enactment of the 1867 Constitution Act. The act united three colonies within the British Empire into a single country called Canada (Iroquoian *kanata* meaning village or land). The entertainment, picnics, barbecues, parades, gatherings with friends, and concluding with fireworks were similar to our familiar American Independence Day celebrations. It was interesting that the two countries had back-to-back patriotic celebrations three days apart. Many American cars lined up at northbound border crossings to celebrate Canada Day, and three days later, the southbound border crossings would be backed up as Canadians flocked to participate in Independence Day celebrations in Seattle (as for our Lower Mainland location). On a couple of special occasions, brothers John and David Ottewell, together with their wives, Myra and Joanne, treated us with a boat ride from their dock at Tsawwassen, British Columbia, into the Strait of Georgia to watch the fireworks launched from neighboring Point Roberts, Washington, USA.

Point Roberts is uniquely located at the tip of the Tsawwassen Peninsula and shares the international border with the Municipality of Delta in British Columbia. Boundary Bay lies to the east of Point Roberts and the Strait of Georgia to the south and west. Point Roberts, measuring two miles from north to south and three miles east to west, has a population of just over 1,200. The pene-exclave (land inaccessible directly to its assigned country without passing through a foreign territory) was created when Great Britain and the United States in the mid-nineteenth century, with the Oregon Treaty, settled the Pacific Northwest border dispute. Both parties agreed that the 49th parallel would define both countries' territories, but the small tip south of the 49th parallel, now known as Point Roberts, was an oversight.

For convenience and efficiency for sending and receiving U.S. mail when we moved to Delta, we maintained a mailbox at the Point Roberts, Washington, post office. Doug typically checked the U.S. mail weekly on his way home from work with a minor inconvenient detour and low-key border crossings, both leaving and returning with a full tank of less expensive U.S. gasoline and a gallon of milk. We waited perhaps a week between trips to pick up or drop off our U.S. mail, but the delay was still more efficient than the delivery of international mail by Canada Post.

When Doug began teaching at the University of British Columbia and Debbie and Sharilyn began their school year, I wanted to have an identity within our neighbourhood. Starting with General Gordon School, where our daughters were students, I inquired about volunteer opportunities. The principal shared his concern for a grade-two child who had recently arrived with his family from Greece. The student was resourceful and eager to participate, but he spoke very little English. Would I help him learn to speak English? I eagerly accepted the challenge. That afternoon, I met Nicholas, his parents, and his teacher. We were a good match. Without the convenience of today's online options, I immediately began researching, clipping pictures, shopping for teaching aids, and planning our sessions. Nicholas and I bonded quickly and met every afternoon. Both he and I enjoyed our ESL dialogues and saw significant progress. I was visibly crushed when after about six weeks, during a follow-up meeting, the principal told me that Nicholas's teacher had reported to him that her student was making noticeable progress, but he was speaking English with a Southern accent. As the principal watched me wilt, he quickly responded, "Oh, please don't stop tutoring Nicholas. I told his teacher not to worry. His family is from *southern* Greece." Nicholas and I competently finished the ten-month Canadian school term together.

Buying Our First Home

The government of British Columbia offered a low-interest second mortgage to assist renters with the purchase of their first home. Qualifications required that applicants had been residents of British Columbia for a minimum of one year. We applied 366 days following our entry into Canada and were immediately approved. Property values within Vancouver were too expensive for frugal first-time buyers, like us, with young families. Gail, one of Doug's colleagues, suggested that we look in the suburb of North Delta, where she had purchased a more reasonably priced house.

Following Gail's advice, we looked, and in September 1972, we found and purchased a newly built modest three-bedroom house on a one-third acre 70 × 205 lot. Being naive about home purchasing, without negotiating, we offered to pay the listed price of $27,900 Canadian mortgaged with our bank and the B. C. Government second mortgage incentive. The back of the lot joined the quiet extensive playground of Hellings Elementary School. Debbie and Sharilyn walked two blocks via the main streets to school rather than the faster over-the-back-fence access. This quelled the temptation for neighbourhood children to use our yard as a street-to-school thoroughfare. Adjoining the open playground was a wooded area that provided easy access and a pleasant walk to Kennedy Heights Shopping Centre.

For the first two weeks of school and before closing on the house in mid-September, I drove our daughters the forty-five-minute trip (on a good day) through the Vancouver suburbs, over the heavily traveled Oak Street Bridge that spanned the north arm of the mighty Fraser River, through the George Massey Tunnel to Hellings

Elementary School, where Sharilyn began grade one and Debbie was in grade four. I spent those school days reading in the food courts of two malls, Surrey Place or Guildford, or at a picnic table in the pastoral setting of Bear Creek Park in the neighbouring Municipality of Surrey.

On moving day from Vancouver to Delta, eight-year-old Debbie, in her efforts and excitement to move her belongings into her own room, gashed her foot on a metal dollhouse. For the first time, I met our next-door neighbours, Don and Jackie Davison, not only asking to use their phone but also to get recommendations for a doctor for our medical emergency. Dr. Wang's new practice was nearby and welcoming new patients. I ran back home, where Doug was holding Debbie with her foot bleeding in the bathtub. At our front door, I met the pastor of the local Baptist church where we had visited the previous Sunday. Being sensitive to the *oh-no* look on my face, Pastor Allen Schmidt considerately asked if he had come at a bad time. I answered affirmatively with the explanation. He had a quick look at Debbie's wound, asked if I had found a doctor, then quickly prayed us on our way to get Debbie's foot stitched. For the second time in one year, she had found our family doctor. We found our first Canadian physician two weeks after arriving in Vancouver when Debbie broke her arm in our backyard while doing gymnastics with her new friends in our neighbourhood.

Pastor Schmidt checked later that week to see how Debbie was progressing. We returned to visit Royal Heights Baptist Church the following Sunday. *Once again, another pivotal event in our lives was aligning ourselves with the just folks of Royal Heights Baptist Church.*

Unaware of the providential plan unfolding around us, Doug and I were enjoying our children, our jobs, our home in Delta, our church, and new friends. My thirtieth birthday came one month after our move from the Kitsilano duplex to Delta. Doug and I had spent that day adding and leveling topsoil to seed the bare lawn. When evening came, we were exhausted and dirty. I was somewhat suspicious when Doug suggested that we celebrate my milestone birthday by going out for ice cream. I am one of the few people who is strangely not particularly fond of ice cream. When I graciously declined, his second and more sensible idea was to shower and refresh ourselves. Soon after cleaning up and enjoying leftovers for family supper, the doorbell rang. Doug smiled as he sent me down the stairs to open the door. There were three couples (Mary and Don Bock, Myra and John Ottewell, and Kay and Ray Maxwell) from our new church who brought gifts, desserts, and games. It was one of my best celebrations ever and the only time I have played Monopoly until after midnight to finish the game.

Soon, other than our Southern accents, we had assimilated well as Canadians. Canadians and Americans embrace the innate lineage that we were "children of a common mother"; however, there are cultural differences in our expected mores. Like most parents in the southern United States, Doug and I had diligently taught our young children to address older people with an appropriate title of respect. Children and adults alike used "sir" and "ma'am" in response to any query by an elder and especially to anyone, regardless of age, in a role of authority. I was regularly admonished by Debbie's and Sharilyn's Canadian schoolteachers that our children's saying "sir" or "ma'am" was perceived by many Canadians to be sarcasm.

Gerry and Darlene Hall, next-door neighbours in our new neighbourhood, were helpful in our transition to our new Canadian culture. While I was still a work in progress, Darlene and I enjoyed a girls' day out, including shopping and lunch. Sensing that Darlene had something on her mind, I asked, "What's wrong?" With discretion and gentleness, she explained that my friendliness toward other shoppers, such as asking for their advice about a particular product or asking the diners at the table next to us if they would recommend the menu item that they seemed to be enjoying was a *faux pas*. Who knew? I just didn't understand how Southern hospitality could be offensive! I genuinely appreciated her counsel. She smiled and said, "I just don't want them to think you are a prostitute." Well, that did it! I became conscientious and *tried* to be more reserved. I don't think I ever totally succeeded. Talking to strangers is how I have always made new friends. Twenty years later, when we moved to Ohio and strangers asked my advice about a particular product or the couple in the restaurant asked from an accompanying table if I would recommend my menu choice, I considered that as "welcome home."

Our North Delta neighbourhood was stable with middle-class working families. Years later, in 1984, Sharilyn graduated from North Delta Senior Secondary School with a number of classmates who had started first grade with her at Hellings Elementary and continued through grades 8 and 10 at Delview Junior Secondary. Completing nine years (grades 3 through 11) in Canadian public schools, Debbie finished her 1981 high school senior year at Clarke Central High School in Athens, Georgia, while Doug was on his first study leave at the University of Georgia from the University of British Columbia. Sharilyn spent her ninth-grade year as a student at Clarke Central in Athens.

Doug, Debbie, Sharilyn, and I fared well living in Delta, a suburb of Vancouver. Doug didn't even object to the nearly one-hour drive each way to UBC. He and his colleague, Gail, alternated driving the unpredictable route through heavy traffic that was notoriously complicated by frequent rain and/or accidents on bridges or in the tunnel. Contrary to what one may think, it seldom snowed on the Lower Mainland; but when snow did come, traffic was slowed or at a standstill. Sufficient snow-clearing equipment was too costly for the Ministry of Transportation to maintain for the rare snow emergencies.

While shopping in our local mall, I yielded to the enticement of a promotional table sponsored by an investment firm. My curiosity drew me close enough to initiate a low-key conversation with an advisor. That evening, Doug and I looked through the brochures that I had collected. We discussed our then-limited investment knowledge and experience. Reassuring myself and Doug that I had a good feeling about Victor's competent no-pressure mall presentation, we phoned the number on his business card. Within a few days, Victor met with us. Both Doug and I felt comfortable and confident to invest a portion of our savings. At the same time, we were anxious about our first experience of investing in the stock market. For at least the next year, we regularly tracked our mutual fund investments in the market indices section of the *Vancouver Sun* newspaper.

During that year, Victor was hired by another investment firm. By that time, he had earned our trust, and we moved our accounts with him to the new firm. That was in the mid-1970s. We still maintain our Canadian retirement accounts with that company. Although the name has changed, their commitment to serve us well and our loyalty to the firm have not.

Connecting to Southern
Baptists in Canada

Southern Baptists were a fledgling denomination in Canada when our family arrived in Vancouver in 1971. The one year that we lived in Vancouver, Doug, Debbie, and I were members of Westlynn Baptist Church in North Vancouver. When we moved to North Delta in 1972, we joined Royal Heights Baptist Church with a congregation of about one hundred, including several families with children the ages of ours. Little did we realize that our affiliation with that church would bond our entire family with those church friends for a lifetime. There was no better place to serve than in a growing, exciting church where we were embraced and accepted: Americans with Southern accents!

Royal Heights Baptist Church, organized in 1967, continued to grow under the capable leadership of Pastor Allen Schmidt and his successors. When we joined, the membership was approximately seventy-five, with perhaps twenty-five regular attendees who were not members. Probably 25 percent of the membership were relocated Americans, as we were. The international church family was not only "Children of a Common Mother" as inscribed on the Peace Arch at the Canadian/United States border; but more importantly, we were children of a Common *Father*.

As I had done at General Gordon Elementary School in Vancouver, I reached out to find a way to become involved in my new North Delta community. In late 1972, I began volunteering in the church office. Royal Heights was rapidly growing beyond not only administrative demands on Pastor Schmidt, but the congregation was also reaching more people than the small building could accommodate. In February 1973, the church hired me as an administrative assistant where I served as executive secretary to Rev. Schmidt in his positions as church pastor, president of the Northwest Baptist Convention, president of the Canadian Southern Baptist Conference, and president of the local Surrey-Delta Ministerial Association. When Pastor Schmidt moved on to become executive director of the Canadian Convention of Southern Baptists, I continued to serve with successive pastors, Eugene Laird and Kim Norwood, at Royal Heights for a total of eleven years.

During my tenure as church secretary, I was regularly involved with annually organizing and planning Vacation Bible School. Many Baptist churches, as well as some other denominations, used VBS literature that was published in the United States. Daily, weather permitting, three excited children were chosen to be bearers of the Canadian flag, the Christian flag, and the Bible to lead the VBS processional of all children and teachers into the sanctuary. The protocol was that the large assembly, before dispersing to appropriate age-group classes, participated in pledging allegiance to the flags and to the Bible. I sensed an awkwardness at the time the American-written program included the pledge of allegiance, and there was no pledge to the Canadian flag prior to the singing of "O Canada" and then continuing to the pledges and anthems for the Christian flag and the Bible. Informed by Pastor Schmidt that Canada did not have an official pledge for their beautiful maple-leaf banner, and with his permission and encouragement, I composed a pledge and offered it to fill the apparent void.

Within a year or so, the pledge that I had written was being used in pockets across Canada and was being pledged in churches, schools, and other venues where Canadians proudly saluted their flag and country, not only in song but now also in a verbal commitment. I regret that I do not have a copy of the pledge that began with the words, "I pledge allegiance to the flag unfurled for Canada, my country..." Ironically, I could not say the pledge that I had written because pledging allegiance to an iconic symbol of another country was one of several acts outlined by the U.S. Department of State that could give cause for the United States government to expatriate a U.S. citizen. Among the acts for which loss of citizenship is prescribed is that of taking an oath of allegiance to a foreign state.

When Royal Heights church members constructed a new building from foundation to spire in 1974, our eight-year-old Sharilyn joined and was one of the first to be baptized in the new sanctuary. She had amused us earlier by saying, after years of playing on churches' cold linoleum floors, that she was not going to become a member of a church until we went to one that had carpet. Doug and I were relieved that Pastor Schmidt counseled Sharilyn about her decision before her baptism to ensure all of us that she had joined for the right reason. Having strong leadership, a new building (with carpet!), and a congregation on mission to introduce their neighbourhood to Christ, the church soon grew to a membership of more than 250 and became the flagship church for Canadian Southern Baptists.

Pastor Laird's wife, Janet, was an accomplished organist. Pastor Laird's brother, who lived in Texas, donated a dual-keyboard church organ and sound system that blessed and empowered the Royal Heights music program. When the Lairds moved elsewhere, Vivian Wilkie capably assumed the role of an organist. Eventually, all our organists had relocated, and our organist pool was depleted. Every workday, I would pass by the organ and stop to admire the beautiful piece of furniture, now silenced from its designated purpose. I began to wonder...could I, with somewhat limited musical ability, learn the functions of the multiple keyboards, stops, and all those pedals? I had previous accompaniment experience by playing piano for worship services at smaller churches, but this endeavor could stretch me a bit. I purchased a beginner's book and stayed after work to privately take on the challenge. Playing to empty pews and halls allowed me to practice and experiment with no inhibitions. I was amazed that in a relatively short time, in my somewhat biased opinion, I moved from practice mode to performance mode.

I enjoyed serving as the church organist for a couple of years before our move to Georgia for Doug's 1987–88 study leave. Musically gifted, Osa Marie, wife of Gerry Wittenmyer, then director of Missions for Capilano Baptist Association, became the church organist. This was the dawning of the era when classic hymns, hymnals, and traditional instruments of accompaniment were segueing to praise teams with guitars, drums, keyboards, and screen monitors.

Numerous Southern Baptist church groups from the United States brought encouragement, inspiration, and motivation when they scheduled mission trips to Canada. They came with music, backyard Bible clubs, leadership training, construction work, VBS volunteers, generous donations, and mission endeavors. Local church congregations were cooperative, even eager, to billet the groups. Young Canadian men and women by the dozens began attending Golden Gate Baptist Seminary in the San Francisco area, Southwestern Seminary in Ft. Worth, and Baptist colleges throughout the United States to train themselves to evangelize their homeland of Canada and beyond.

I was privileged and honored to have been elected to two three-year terms as one of twelve members to serve on the historic first executive board for the Canadian Convention of Southern Baptists. It was a compelling responsibility that I took seriously and executed passionately. Amazing opportunities ensued as the newly elected board met in October 1985 in Toronto with directors of the various agencies of the Nashville-based Southern Baptist Convention to iron out details and strategies for birthing the Canadian Convention of Southern Baptists. The growing denomination was more appropriately renamed the Canadian National Baptist Convention in 2008.

Canadian Southern Baptists strategically planned their annual Canadian Conference in May of 1986 in Victoria, British Columbia, to coincide with the opening of the Expo Celebration (World's Fair) in Vancouver, May 2 through October 13. Transportation by BC Ferry across the Georgia Strait from Swartz Bay near Victoria on Vancouver Island to Tsawwassen near Vancouver is a spectacular 1.5-hour cruise. The deliberate scheduling and venue were planned to accommodate messengers from across Canada who would likely piggyback attending the conference with the Expo Celebration. This conference was momentous for Canadian Southern Baptists as the messengers ambitiously voted not only to organize into our own convention but also to commit to the financial challenge to buy property, build, staff, and promote a seminary. The executive board was commissioned to proceed with locating and purchasing a building site for a Canadian-based seminary. Today, the convention headquarters and the Canadian Baptist Theological Seminary and College are located on that chosen site overlooking the beautiful Bow River Valley in Cochrane, Alberta, near Calgary. The seminary provides training for many men and women who are called into Christian ministry, and it is the designated charity to receive memorial donations at my demise and also at Doug's demise.

Trips South:
Family Visits, Study Leaves,
and Providential Intervention

Staying connected with our extended families situated diagonally across the United States took some effort on everyone's part. Long-distance phone calls between Canada and the United States were available at a reduced rate compared to calls to other countries. We paid by the minute and could talk at a cheaper rate on Saturdays and Sundays. Unless there was family news in the South that needed our immediate attention, the calls were typically generated weekly by Doug or me from Canada. Cordless phones had not been invented, nor were speakerphones available. This meant everyone involved in the conversation was confined to one central location, and the corded phone was handed from one person to the next. The first time that we saw a mobile phone was in the Telecom Canada Pavilion at the 1986 World Exhibition in Vancouver. Because of its large size, the invention was demonstrated and marketed as a "car" phone.

We planned our trips to Alabama to occur every year and a half. This schedule worked for us to drive the summer trips when the weather would not likely be a concern. Our family of four, plus our dog, used those cross-country trips to visit many memorable and educational sites. Eighteen months later, we chose to fly, which was more expensive but gave us more uninterrupted time with our fathers in the winter. Summer was peak season for both our dads:

Doug's father, a farmer; mine, manager of Whitfield's cucumber brine station.

Nighttime was ideal for Doug and me to share late driving while the children slept. The traffic was lighter and the temperature cooler. Doug designed a platform that fit over the rear floorboard hump and converted into a cot for Sharilyn. Debbie stretched out on the back seat. We stopped late at motels for rest and baths or showers to refresh us for the next day's travel. There was no included breakfast, continental or otherwise. We ate breakfast at McDonald's or from the previous day's grocery market purchase of milk, cereal, and fruit that was kept cool in our ice chest. At lunchtime, we would scout out a park or picnic area to make sandwiches from deli fixings, followed by a walk and a power nap. On one such stop near Albuquerque, we were serenaded by a mariachi band for our dining enjoyment and relaxation. Supper was a special occasion at a family restaurant. The repertoire of songs that came from our daughters in the back seat included "Country Roads," "Sixteen Tons," "Rhinestone Cowboy," "All the Gold in California," and "Miss Mary Mack."

The three-thousand-mile trip (before cell phones) with two children, a dog, and our Canadian Automobile Association (CAA) TripTik created anxiety for our families, who were awaiting our safe arrival. For our traveling safety, my dad gave us a citizens' band (CB) radio that he had rebuilt. Used mostly by truckers, the land mobile radio system provided short-distance communication. We are thankful that we never had to use the system for an emergency, but it was entertaining for Debbie (whose "handle" was Eskimo Pie) and Sharilyn (Strawberry Shortcake) and also for Doug and me, as the girls chatted with truckers who were driving in our reception area. The truckers seemed to enjoy it too, often honking their loud air-horns and waving as they passed.

Every seventh year during Doug's tenure at UBC, he was eligible for a school-year study leave drawing 75 percent of his annual pay in Canadian dollars. For both study leaves (1980–1981 and 1987–1988), we returned to Athens, Georgia. Doug had connections at the University of Georgia who provided office space and some staff support within the Mathematics Education Department. From our having lived in Athens from 1968–1971 while Doug was a student, we had established an amicable level of comfort within the area. Plus, Athens was a somewhat convenient five-hour drive to Atmore, Alabama, allowing us to reconnect frequently with hometown family and friends.

The 1980–1981 school year was Debbie's high school senior year. If Doug took his leave at this time, Debbie would not graduate from North Delta Secondary School with those who had been her Canadian classmates since grade four. Doug discussed the timing of his potential leave with Debbie before applying. Indicating her willingness to return to Athens and even with excitement that she could graduate with some classmates from her first-grade class, Doug proceeded with and was granted his request for study leave.

A number of Canadian friends treated me to a farewell lunch just prior to our year away. That morning, Doug and I had continued our interior painting to ready the house for the coming year's renters. I had not complained to anyone about my more frequent and more intense chest pains. During our lunch, one observant friend whispered to ask if I was okay. Since I was the honoree and not wanting to be a party pooper, I responded yes. Following the luncheon, I immediately drove to my doctor's office nearby. It was a blessing that Dr. Wang was on vacation, and I saw a temporary fill-in physician. Dr. Wang had been our family doctor since 1972 when he stitched Debbie's gashed foot on move-in day to our Delta home. I concluded that he was a good doctor, but with my Southern accent, he never understood what I told him about my health concerns and symptoms. Likewise, I never understood his Cantonese-accent diagnosis nor how to treat the issue. We got along very well.

The interim physician examined me and said, "I am sending you to hospital.[1] Check in at the emergency-room entrance. A cardiologist will meet you there. If he confirms what I hear, you will be admitted to hospital." Not having a convenient way to communicate with Doug, plus having quite an independent spirit and not

---

[1]   Canadian/British English typically omits the article *the* before the word *hospital.*

wanting to interrupt Doug's pressing paint project, I followed the doctor's instructions. The assigned cardiologist was waiting for me, confirmed the pericarditis diagnosis, and told me I was being admitted to the intensive care unit (ICU). My response was "Okay, but I can't stay long because I am moving to Georgia in two weeks." I shall never forget the stunned look on his face.

His reply was "Mrs. Owens, I am not inviting you to a dance. I am admitting you to the ICU." Surrey Memorial Hospital's emergency room receptionist was a member of our Royal Heights church. One can only imagine the disbelief when Doug received the call from her with the shocking news. He thought I was partying with "the girls." Instead, I spent a couple of days in the ICU, followed by a few more days recovering in a hospital room. Because the sound of my heart beating against the inflamed pericardium was so clearly pronounced and easily identifiable, medical students, with my permission, came regularly as a class with their stethoscopes to listen to what they called "the rub." On a positive note, we departed for Georgia on schedule, and help came from the men of the church to finish painting the house interior.

Church friends, David and Joanne Ottewell, sold us their nearly new travel trailer. Not only had David's mother's waterfront home become available for them, but also David and Joanne realized that a travel trailer did not allow enough personal space even for newlyweds. We packed the spacious trailer with adequate clothing and personal belongings for one year.

We had not found a place to live in Athens when we launched our journey from Vancouver. Along the way, Doug phoned Dr. James W. (Jim) Wilson, Mathematics Education Department chair at UGA, to update him on our estimated arrival schedule. During the conversation, Doug inquired of Jim if he knew of available housing. Jim immediately put us in contact with Dr. Mike Mahaffey. Dr. Mahaffey, one of the professors involved years earlier during Doug's University of Georgia doctoral program, had scheduled his 1980–1981 leave to teach in Bermuda. Understandably, Dr. Mahaffey was concerned about leaving his lovely, completely furnished two-story home in the Athens' Five Points community. Both he and our family were relieved that we could live in and care for his house while paying a modest rent plus utilities. We parked our travel trailer in Athens at our rented home that had become available perfectly timed for our arrival.

Our priority was to become involved with a church as much as one year would permit. Being a mom, I especially desired to find a church that had an active youth program: camps, choirs, hand-bells, and mission trips. On our first Sunday in town, we attended Sunday school and worship service at Beech Haven Baptist Church, where our prior connection had been eleven years earlier when Deb was in the church's kindergarten, and Sharilyn was in the preschool program. A couple of women who greeted us excitedly announced Beech Haven's imminent plans to begin a deaf ministry. It seemed that everything was in place, including deaf participants, and the church was aggressively trying to find a sign-language interpreter. Doug and I were speechless and somewhat hesitant to reveal that our sixteen-year-old Debbie was a fluent American Sign Language (ASL) interpreter, having worked in our Canadian church's deaf ministry, deaf youth camps, and missions. The following week, our new friends, Kitty and Pam, visited our home to welcome us back to our year in Athens, and they asked if we had questions about Beech Haven. We shared that all our feelings about the church were pos-itive, but we wanted to visit at least a couple more churches before prayerfully deciding where to be involved for just one year. *Another pivotal moment was when Kitty politely stated, "We have poured out our hearts in prayer for an interpreter for our deaf congregation. God has sent us Debbie. We really hope to see you next Sunday."* They did. We did. Debbie did. One month later, the deaf congregation was going strong and had organized a deaf choir.

In early 1981, Kitty asked me to attend two weeks of intensive sign-language classes with her at the Bill Rice Ranch in Murfreesboro, Tennessee. This training not only positively impacted my ability to communicate with the deaf, but also gave me the insight to interpret what had previously been the means of secret communication used by our teenage daughters when they chose to exclude their parents from their conversations.

ON THE SHOULDERS OF JUST FOLKS

Greg and his Bennett family were longtime members of Beech Haven Baptist Church. Even now, when he returns with us to the church for a visit, Greg always looks down the hall, and he remembers the first time his eyes met Debbie's on our first visit. Seven years later in 1987, Debbie married Greg, who is still the love of her life. When Doug and I were considering a permanent retirement location, memories of Beech Haven tipped our decision favoring Athens.

Debbie and Greg established themselves in Columbus, Georgia. Greg retired in 2015 from thirty years as a lexicographer at the Western Hemisphere Institute for Security Cooperation (WHINSEC) at Ft. Benning. At his retirement, Greg was presented the Superior Civilian Service Medal, one of the highest honors bestowed on federal employees. Debra was also honored by the U.S. Department of Defense for her role in supporting WHINSEC, formerly the School of the Americas. The surprise recognition was presented to her in 2002 by the commandant of the institute. Debra retired at the end of the 2021 school year after thirty years of investing her gifted teaching skills while working with special needs students in Clarke and Muskogee (Georgia) counties. Two of Debra's prestigious awards as an educator were "Giving Your Best" award presented by a local TV station for her work with people who are deaf and her receipt of "Teacher of the Year" award.

Debbie in twelfth grade and Sharilyn in ninth grade experienced their first classes in American history at Clarke Central High School in Athens. The stories connected to American holidays that they heard from me year after year in Canada when the U.S. flag became our dining table centrepiece was what they knew about their birth country. In her general science class, Sharilyn tackled the U.S. customary system of measures that year, another first for her. During our years in Canada, our family learned and functioned well using the International System of Measures (SI Metric). We regretted that Sharilyn, at age fourteen and as a ninth-grader, had to put aside metric for this one year. The metric system had been embraced by the rest of the world except for the United States, Liberia, and Myanmar. Sharilyn quickly rebounded to metric when returning to Canada for grade 10. As I write this recollection of her ninth-grade

133

"setback," Sharilyn currently has an earned doctorate in mathematics education from the University of Tennessee and serves as executive director of Strategic Innovation and Effectiveness at Forsyth Technical Community College in Winston-Salem, North Carolina. Apparently, no long-term mathematical dysfunction occurred.

I enrolled for the 1980–81 school year at UGA and welcomed the opportunity and my personal challenge as a thirty-eight-year-old wife and mother of two active teenagers. I maintained my grade A goal and achieved the desired status of inclusion on the dean's list. I looked forward to hosting and entertaining guests, including school and church friends of our popular daughters, in our lovely rental home.

Our Canadian pastor, Allen Schmidt, detoured to Athens to visit us while he was attending a conference in Atlanta. When we realized that Allen's scheduled visit to Athens would be not only on Sunday but also on Mother's Day 1981, we asked Beech Haven's deacons if he could preach. Beech Haven was without a pastor at that time. Of course, with Allen's high-profile credentials and with their confidence in our recommendation, the deacons complied. Allen delivered a memorable Mother's Day message on the godly and maternal virtues of Mary, Jesus's mother.

Another memorable event of our 1980–1981 year in Athens was the release of American hostages who had been held captive in Iran. The fifty-two hostages, seized from the U.S. Embassy in Tehran in November 1979, were finally released on January 20, 1981, after having been held for 444 days. With the completion of negotiations, our elated family watched as TV breaking news announced that the hostages had been released. At the moment President Ronald Reagan completed his twenty-minute inaugural address after being sworn in to succeed President James Earl "Jimmy" Carter, the fifty-two American hostages were released to U.S. personnel. In an exemplary gesture of statesmanship, President Reagan sent former President Carter to greet the released hostages. Athens, along with the free world, planned celebratory events. Within a day or two, I attended the ecumenical thanksgiving service downtown, where Christians and Jews alike joined in praise and worship. I have Psalm 116 noted in my Bible as the passage appropriately read by the rabbi during that service.

A year earlier, on January 28, 1980, six of the U.S. employees at the Embassy, who had miraculously evaded capture by hiding in the Canadian Embassy, flew out of Tehran using fake Canadian passports issued by order of Canada's Prime Minister, Joe Clark. Their rescue from Iran was cleverly known as the Canadian Caper. We Owenses, not yet dual citizens, felt the pride that both our countries had cooperated to effectively pull this off. I remember seeing American tourists in Vancouver wearing "Thank you, Canada!" T-shirts. Yes, *siblings*! As inscribed on the Peace Arch frieze: "Children of a Common Mother."

Being avid college football fans, we could not have picked a better study-leave year than 1980 to be "between the hedges" at Sanford Stadium. The University of Georgia Bulldogs, coached by Vince Dooley, finished their 1980 season 12–0 overall and 6–0 in the Southeastern Conference. Thanks to freshman and all-time great running back, Herschel Walker, and University of Georgia's team with a late win over Notre Dame in the Sugar Bowl, the Bulldogs won the 1980 national championship title. Forty-one years later, the Bulldogs, coached by Kirby Smart, earned the 2021 championship title by defeating the University of Alabama Crimson Tide at 33–18.

Returning to Life and
Responsibilities in Canada

After Debbie received her acceptance to enter the University of Georgia as a freshman in September 1981, she returned with our family to British Columbia in August to say goodbye to her Canadian friends. Because Debbie had lived in Georgia the year prior and had been issued a Georgia driver's license, she qualified as a Georgia resident. We were thankful that she (we) was not required to pay out-of-state fees. Nevertheless, there were books, meals, lodging, and related living expenses.

To help with the costs, I applied for and was hired in October 1981 to fill the position of senior executive secretary to the president of an upstart hotel chain. Initially, the chain was comprised of seven British Columbia hotels that were aggressively being groomed for launching into a much larger chain of luxury accommodations. The business was located near downtown Vancouver. My 8:00 a.m. start time required that I catch the 6:30 a.m. BC Transit bus in suburban North Delta. My workday ended at 5:00 p.m. My North Delta-bound bus dropped me about three blocks from home at 6:30 p.m. Depending on Sharilyn's after-school activities, she often had supper prepared from our preplanned menu.

The firm had already established itself as a catering provider delivering meals to the oil sands and other remote work camps across Canada. I was hired as senior executive secretary to the president and to the operations manager. I also worked closely with the company's vice president, who was the president's son. We all worked well as a

136

team to lay the groundwork and plan the early stages to establish and advance the hotel chain. The hotel staff worked in the same building with the catering operations staff, who occupied about two-thirds of the one-level office space. All staff shared the same break room, giving an opportunity to develop friendships between employees within both entities. There was an amiable relationship among the estimated twenty-five employees for the two businesses.

The office of the operations manager was accessible only by entering the reception suite that encompassed my work area. Eventually, it became obvious that the vice president's female assistant was a frequent visitor to the hotel wing of offices. Having plenty of responsibilities on which to focus my attention, I cordially exchanged greetings with her as she entered and exited the reception area occupied solely by me.

One day, the operations manager approached my desk with an envelope containing a large amount of cash that he said he had received from the manager of the smallest of the hotels that was located in northern British Columbia. I thought it was strange that he asked if I could store the cash temporarily in a safe place until he could deposit it. For the short term, he and I agreed to put the envelope containing the cash in the respective hotel's file folder. He then locked the file cabinet that only either of the two of us could access with our respective keys. He went on his way out of the office to have lunch or attend a meeting. I sat at my desk, processing what had just happened, and I began to see a scheme brewing that was apparently setting me up. Within minutes, I made a rare visit to the vice president's desk to ask if there was a vault in his office suite. Puzzled at my question, he answered affirmatively. I told him that I was feeling uneasy, and I shared the bizarre story about how the cash had been placed in my office file cabinet. As he walked with me down the hall to my office, he prudently said, "So you think the cash is going to disappear, and you will be accused…?" I said yes. I accompanied the vice president back to his safe, where I watched as he turned the combination to secure the envelope. I remained silent about this intervention when the operations manager returned. It was probably the next day, without my being present, that he had looked for the cash that I had assumed he was planning to remove and accuse me. When he questioned me, I calmly replied that the vice president had locked the cash securely in his office vault. I shall never forget the look on his face when the operations manager realized that his plan had been foiled. Meanwhile, the apparent office romance continued.

I received excellent commendations on my July 30, 1982 "Review of Employee Performance" with the office manager. He highlighted numerous accolades with no negative comments nor any areas of my work needing improvement. I was given a raise plus a bonus trip for Doug and me to the company's hotel property on Vancouver Island. Doug and I were also treated to a gratis sports-fishing trip. On December 1, 1982, four months after my rave review, the company president for whom I worked was out of town. The operations manager came to my desk and gave me notice to collect my personal belongings because he had authorization from the company president to dismiss me effective immediately. Senior staff and fellow employees in both the catering and hotel subsidiaries of the business were in shock when the news of my firing made its rounds. The only explanation to which I could connect my dismissal was the questionable friendship that I had regularly observed between the operations manager and the vice president's assistant, each married to someone else. I had not shared my suspicions with anyone except Doug. Being unjustly and abruptly fired was, until then, the most devastating event of my life. I sobbed and remained in bed for days.

I was numb when my friend and coworker, Lydia, drove me home that day rather than permit me to ride the bus. Lydia, her husband, Lumer, and baby, Irene, had escaped as refugees from Czechoslovakia fourteen years earlier during the Soviet invasion, leaving with only the clothes they wore plus a small suitcase with necessities for their baby. They had left all: family, their house, their invaded homeland, and successful careers to flee to a free country where they did not speak the language. Lydia and her family had experienced far greater emotional trauma than I could ever imagine.

Meanwhile, Dr. Henry Blackaby, a Canadian pastor in Saskatoon, had moved with his family to North Delta when Henry came to assume his position as director of missions for the Capilano

Baptist Association. Doug and I had met the Blackaby family at various Baptist conferences in western Canada. Now living in our community, the Blackabys became members of Royal Heights Baptist Church. Henry was aware of my competence and longevity as administrative assistant to several pastors and my organizing associational and convention meetings, including organizing our Canadian churches' participation with the Northwest Baptist Convention in their hosting the Southern Baptist Convention's 1973 annual meeting in Portland, Oregon, with more than 8,800 attending. Henry didn't blink when he learned of my recent dismissal from my previous position, but he considered it to be God's perfect timing. He offered me the job as his secretary while he transitioned to Baptist grass-roots connections within the Capilano Association. Frankly, I was perfect for the job. During the time I worked for Henry, his office was in the basement of the Blackaby home. I was frequently invited to share lunch upstairs prepared by Henry's wife and eventually my very good friend, Marilynn. Our teenage daughter, Sharilyn, became Henry's sidekick as the two of them traveled on Sundays to various churches throughout the Lower Mainland of British Columbia. Henry preached and Sharilyn played piano as the local congregations sang praise choruses and hymns of worship. One may recognize Henry's name as the author of *Experiencing God* in addition to numerous other books he has coauthored with his sons and others.

Sadness: Deaths of My Stepfather and Precious Mammaw

I flew to Shreveport to be with Mother when my stepfather died in March of 1982. Johnny had experienced declining health issues after having been transferred in February from the tropical climate of Guam to the frigid temperatures of North Dakota. His failing health forced him to retire earlier than he had planned from his distinguished Air Force career, which included serving in World War II, Korean War, and the Vietnam War. Mother and Johnny had bought a home in Bossier City (Shreveport), Louisiana, conveniently located near Barksdale Air Force Base. At Johnny's funeral in Meridian, Mississippi, I saw his adult children for the first time since 1951 when I was eight years old and under Mother's temporary custody. The relationship between the children and their dad had been strained and with little communication since his divorce from their mother in the late 1940s.

Following Johnny's death, Mother's behavior became more impulsive than ever. Every time I received a call from her prefaced by "Guess what I did today?" I held my breath and braced myself as I prepared for her eccentric response. The first shocker was when Mother, after the fact, informed family that she had Johnny's casket exhumed in Meridian and transported 170 miles for burial in her family's church cemetery plot in Castleberry, Alabama. On the heels of that news came her announcement that she had found an apartment in Ft. Walton Beach, Florida, and was moving from her deeply rooted comfort zone in the Shreveport area. She had listed her Bossier

City home with a realtor and sold it to the first potential buyer's offer on its initial day on the market. Her Ft. Walton Beach residency lasted only a few weeks. When she found ants in her condo, she returned to Shreveport, moving into an apartment complex. Doug and I, living in Ohio, were relieved when in 1993, Mother finally settled in Mobile closer to her siblings, nieces, and nephews.

Mother adjusted quickly and well to Mobile, where she lived out her remaining twenty-one years.

Faye and Mother

I did receive at least one more memorable "Guess-what-I-did-today?" call. Mother was walking to her car from her hairdresser appointment in Mobile. When she passed the Baldwin piano store, she noticed a sign in the window promoting their Christmas piano sale. She bought one, and it had been delivered to her apartment wrapped with a "huge Christmas bow." She proudly announced that she had paid to have my name engraved on a plaque and attached to the back of the piano. Mother, being self-taught, seldom played the piano. Since I already owned a piano and was living 850 miles away in Ohio, when Mother passed, I gave her Baldwin spinet to our daughter, Debra.

Mammaw was approaching ninety-four years of age. For most of those years, she had enjoyed remarkably good health. Later in life, she lost most of her eyesight and hearing. Consequently, she was unable to read, watch television, or easily interact with her visitors.

Her son, Aubrey, and daughter-in-law, Eunice, had become her care-givers and had taken her into their home located on the property next door that Mammaw had given to them. When Uncle Aubrey and Aunt Eunice moved 25 miles away to a lakeside home in Bay Minette, Alabama, they sold the property that had been owned by Pawpaw and/or Mammaw since 1937 and moved Mammaw with them. When Mammaw's health became more fragile, she was admitted to the hospital. Doug and I got the news of her decline, and I immediately flew to Alabama to see her. When I arrived, hospital staff, knowing of my relationship with her, allowed me into the intensive care unit for what would be our last goodbye. Mammaw was aware of my presence as I leaned over her frail body. She wiped the tears from my cheeks so she could, for one last time, kiss the pain away. I had that one final opportunity to try to convey my appreciation for what she and Pawpaw had done for me. There were no adequate words.

Faye and Mammaw

Debbie, a student at the University of Georgia, shared a house in Athens with three girls from South Carolina. The other three room-mates had been friends since childhood. With spring break approaching, Debbie asked if she could invite Mary, Kay, and Melanie to our home in the Vancouver area. In no time, we were planning events, sightseeing trips, and meals to enjoy during their visit. Sharilyn was in grade 11. She eagerly joined in planning a welcome party to include neighbourhood teenagers. In the final preparation for the arrival of Debbie and her friends, the dreaded call came from my dad and stepmom that Mammaw had passed. Her homegoing left a huge void in my life. I no longer had access to the second most significant adult in my life. Dad, Beryl, and Doug helped me process our upcoming plans: my greatest responsibility was to my daughters and the planned events for entertaining Debbie's roommates. All reassured me that my surprise visit to see Mammaw two weeks earlier encouraged her physically and emotionally. When Debbie and her friends arrived at the airport gate in Seattle, I handed Debbie a white rose. Her immediate response was "Mammaw died?" We embraced and cried and then moved on, just as Mammaw would have wanted.

Plans for Expo 1986: Bittersweet

Dad and Beryl visited us in January 1983 just as the hype was revving up surrounding the long-anticipated, well-planned, and organized 1986 Expo Celebration in Vancouver. Dad loved the thrill associated with attending a carnival. He and I had never given a second thought about riding together the biggest and most suspenseful thrillers on the midway. When our British Columbia premier, Bill Bennett, notified his constituents to send to his office names and addresses of friends and relatives around the world, Doug and I did just that. Beryl told us that when she and Daddy received their official invitation to the exhibition from the office of British Columbia's premier, he proudly showed it around in their Atmore circles. Daddy began counting the days until he could experience the touted adventures awaiting at Expo '86. Like a little kid waiting for Christmas, Dad immediately began to make travel plans, including what would be appropriate to pack for the anticipated trip.

The phone call came from my brother-in-law, Roger, on the evening of November 16, 1985. When Roger asked if Doug was there with me, I braced myself for bad news. Dad, age sixty-nine, had died suddenly at home that evening after he and Beryl had spent a fun day Christmas shopping in Pensacola. Collecting myself emotionally, I quickly packed, booked a flight, and flew to Atlanta on November 17. Debbie, in her first year of teaching in Athens, and Sharilyn, a student at the University of Georgia, picked me up at the airport. We proceeded on the four-hour drive in the darkness to south Alabama. In route, the three of us ate supper that Debbie had packed, and we drove the last two-hour leg of the trip through dense fog, arriving around midnight in Atmore for the early morning family viewing prior to Daddy's funeral at Brooks Memorial Baptist Church. Burial followed in the family plot at Oak Hill Cemetery.

Dad's somber discussion with me on my last visit to Atmore as the two of us meandered through Oak Hill Cemetery was regarding his concern that Doug and I could die in another country. What were our plans should one or both of us died in Canada? When I showed him the plots that Doug and I had purchased there at Oak Hill in Atmore, he wisely advised that when the deluge of rushing water from frequent heavy rains channeled its way through the graveyard, our plots were in the flood zone. When I returned there for his burial about a month later, Beryl, now widowed, gave me the two remaining plots of their four for the final resting place for Doug and me. Beryl's son, Ron, already had a plot in the Gantt family plot near Andalusia, Alabama, with his wife, Rose. Next to Dad and Beryl, Dad's oldest brother, Vernon, and sister-in-law, Margaret, are buried in two of their four plots. My cousin, Sandra, who is married to Doug's brother, will be buried along with Roger at the feet of her parents. Continuing the family burial plots, adjacent to Vernon, Margaret, Roger, and Sandra are the burial sites for Vernon and Margaret's older daughter, Gloria, and her husband, Merton Middleton. A stone's throw away are the graves of Marshall and Vernon's brother, Aubrey, and his wife, Eunice.

Vancouver's 1986 Expo Celebration, showcasing the world, opened in May 1986 with all the fanfare and grandiose celebration to be expected for the long-anticipated event. All those invitations that the Premier sent to the addresses that Doug and I provided brought guests streaming to our home for the five-month duration of the fair. While I managed to get clean sheets on the guest beds, Doug was shuttling the departing guests to Seattle airport (where domestic flights were cheaper than flying internationally into Vancouver) and returning with our next carload of Expo attendees. By the fair's end in October, I was ready to conclude that I had mistakenly assumed that *hospitality* was one of my spiritual gifts.

Beryl's trip from Atmore to attend Expo '86 and to be with us to celebrate her fifty-seventh birthday in June was bittersweet. She had navigated the airports and made her flight connections alone, which was a stretch for her. Dad had always been overly protective to the point that, Beryl admitted after his death, she did not know how to pump gas into the car nor how to change a light bulb. Dad's absence at Expo was obviously poignant. We all missed his adventurous spirit. To celebrate Beryl's June 28 birthday, we ate dinner at the Top of Vancouver revolving restaurant. That alone was a once-in-a-lifetime thrill for a dear woman from the small crossroads town of Perdido, Alabama.

Faye and Stepmom Beryl

Beryl died in 2014 at the age of eighty-four. She grieved Dad's death the remaining twenty-nine years that she lived as his widow.

Doug's Uncle Lawrence and Aunt Chestine drove diagonally across the United States in their camper van with Doug's parents from the Atmore area to Vancouver so that the four of them could experience the Exposition. Doug's mother, Verta, was eleven years old when her mother died a few days after giving birth to Uncle Lawrence. Verta, being the second oldest child and the only female in the family, took on the responsibilities of an adult, raising her younger siblings. Bruce Grimes, brother of the deceased mother, adopted his newborn nephew, and Lawrence's last name became Grimes rather than Timothy, the surname of his birth family.

Second Study Leave: Preparation for Job Opportunity in Canada

During the 1987–88 school year, Doug and I returned to the University of Georgia for his second study leave. We moved into a three-bedroom duplex in Athens with Sharilyn that she had shared with Debbie prior to Debbie and Greg's June 20 wedding. Unlike the 1980–1981 study leave, I did not enjoy the luxury of being a UGA college student. With Debbie's wedding three months earlier and Sharilyn's approaching June wedding, I applied for part-time work, hoping that an employer would hire me, although I would be available to work for less than one year before returning to Vancouver.

Following advice from local friends, I applied for positions through the Department of Human Resources (HR) at the University of Georgia. Human Resources gave me details of two part-time openings: one in the Business Economics Department and the other, working with a team on a doctoral leadership grant, "Planning a Needs Assessment Management System (PANAMS)," in the Division for the Education of Exceptional Children. The job description of the latter appealed to me; however, when I interviewed, the position had already been offered to another applicant. I did think it was strange that interviews continued if the position was no longer available. The following day, when offered the part-time job in the Business Economics Department, I reluctantly accepted. Within a week, I knew that this position was a good fit for me. Dr. Dusansky, department chair, his administrative secretary, Judy Griffin (my supervisor), four other support staff, and ten professors warmly welcomed me into the department.

I was competent in my new job, fitting in, and daily looking forward to my 1:00 p.m. start time. After one week, a call from Human Resources personnel informed me that the grant position opening that I had so desired was again available. The first person had not worked out. The grant principal investigator hoped that I was still interested and available. Interested? *Yes*. Available? *No*. I explained to the HR person that I had planned to work only part-time. I added that I had earlier been extremely interested in working on the research grant. Her astonishing advice was "Would you con-sider working mornings on the grant project and continue working afternoons in the Department of Economics for a week or so and then choose the one you prefer?" Okay. That's what I did for two weeks. Enjoying both jobs and working environments, I worked the entire year: mornings on the grant and lunch in the car while driving to the Business Economics Department to work in the afternoons. Both of my UGA positions energized me professionally and together were unknowingly preparing me for employment upon my arrival back in Vancouver that fall.

At this point, I was oblivious that my extensive training plus the experience of using the MultiMate word-processing program were laying the groundwork for my next job opportunity awaiting my return to British Columbia. For the first time, it was now just the two of us settling back into our North Delta home in the fall of 1988. I soon began looking for employment. When we moved to Georgia a year earlier, I had advised my church personnel committee that I did not plan to resume the secretarial position when I returned in a year. Other than my recent year as an employee at the University of Georgia, my work experience, for the most part, had been limited to church administrative and organizational skills. I was given an apti-tude test by an employment placement agency in the Vancouver area to evaluate my abilities. My resulting tentative job placement was with Island Paper Mills as secretary to the company president while his administrative assistant was on maternity leave. This assignment was working out well, and I thought I was possibly being groomed for a permanent position.

My phone rang. The voice on the other end of the call was the person who had administered the occupational skills tests when I had applied earlier with the placement agency. Her first question was "What is *MultiMate?*" Her agency had received a request from a prestigious land-services firm whose objectives were to ensure that property owners were fairly compensated when their real estate was expropriated by the government, or their businesses disrupted in part or in whole for public use. The public-domain process was accomplished by thorough forensic real-estate appraisals and documentation with all reports compiled using the Multimate word-processing program. The placement agency had only one applicant with the required exceptional knowledge of Multimate. *Me!* My UGA positions had groomed me to be market-ready and proficient in providing computer processing, investigative, project coordination, and paralegal assistance. These were the required credentials for me to be the successful candidate hired to work side by side with clients, government agents, lawyers, and expert witnesses in my new position with Interwest Property Services Ltd. and Fraser Land Services Inc.

On a rare snow-day event on February 14, 1990, I left my workplace at Interwest in New Westminster at day's end and balked at the snow-covered walkway to my car on the top level of the parking ramp that partially extended over the mighty Fraser River. Returning to my office, I phoned to get permission to leave my car in the parkade until weather conditions improved to drive safely. En route to the bus stop to ride home, I met a crowd of pedestrians making their way to the bumper-to-bumper, traffic-jammed Pattullo Bridge. I joined the procession when they informed me that all buses were at a standstill in congested snowbound traffic. With confidence that there was power in numbers, we entered the narrow pedestrian walkway crossing through the arch bridge alongside the impatient drivers. I recall the event well. Just five months earlier, I had become a grandmother with the birth and miraculous survival of our first grandchild, Thomas. I boasted to my walking companions, strangers now friends, as we trudged the snow ascending the steep Scott Road hill, that I was doing well for a grandma on a five-mile (eight-kilometer) hike in the six-inch (fifteen-centimeter) snowfall.

The birth of our grandson, Thomas, referenced above was indeed a miracle. On the evening of September 6, 1989, our pregnant daughter, Debra, became concerned when she had not felt her previously very active baby move for at least a day. Debra was already scheduled for a caesarean section on September 8 due to the baby's transverse-breach position. The doctor met Debra and Greg at the hospital. When the baby did not respond to stress tests, Thomas was delivered by C-section that night. Several specialists were in attendance. The umbilical cord was wrapped around his neck at least nine times. Oxygen was required to start the lungs functioning for the seven-pound, four-ounce marvel. I flew from Vancouver to Georgia to assist in any way possible. Doug joined me three weeks later, when we all celebrated Thomas's well-being and wondered about God's future plans for His and our miracle baby.

My employment at Interwest Property Services Ltd. with partners Danny, Brian, David, and Mario was advantageous to Doug and me during the subdivision and marketing of our personal property. The new Alex Fraser Bridge, a cable-stayed steel structure over the Fraser River, was completed in 1986, connecting Richmond and New Westminster with North Delta. By shortening the travel time and driving distance into Vancouver, the opening of the bridge stimulated development in our North Delta and neighbouring Surrey suburbs. Compliant with the 1984 agreement between Britain and China, Hong Kong was to be handed over to communist China on July 1, 1997, after 156 years of British rule. This fear brought an influx of Hong Kong residents who were anxious about the potential political impact. Thousands were desperately seeking to buy property and move anywhere, particularly to the Vancouver area that boasted the second-largest Chinese community on the continent; San Francisco's Chinatown ranking number one.

Prior to widespread knowledge of the imminent housing boom, Doug and I were approached by a developer who offered a higher than the market value price for our property. Somewhat flattered and already considering purchasing a larger house, we accepted the offer.

When I proudly announced the news of our negotiations, Mario, senior partner at Interwest, was alarmed and informed us that our purchaser had bought with the intent to subdivide. Purchasing with the intent to flip was legal, but Mario knew from his circle of informants that our property was on the verge of even greater value. Other than angst being the emotional price that Doug and I paid, Mario's expertise and the help of the company's corporate attorneys were gratis. Amazingly, they succeeded in getting us released from the sales contract.

As Vancouver and the western coast of North America braced for the blitz of property buyers fleeing Hong Kong, neighbours on our quiet 86th Avenue corridor which conveniently connected our street to Scott Road, a main thoroughfare to Kennedy Heights Shopping Centre, the Municipality of Surrey, and beyond, began to strategize. Most of the properties on the north side of 86th Avenue had deep lots like ours, and subdivisions by property owners became a popular venture. The Zoning and Planning Department of Delta reluctantly issued permits for the divisions allowing the awkwardness of a rear property accessed by a driveway alongside the existing front house. Our property had the necessary 205-foot depth, but the 70-foot frontage was not adequate to allow for a driveway to the rear.

We had put aside the thought of any possibility of subdividing until our neighbor, an immigrant from India, approached us in 1989 with his brainstorm. Dalip had the required frontage, but he did not know how, nor did he want to attempt, to navigate the complicated legal system with which he was not familiar. He offered to give access to both his and our potential rear lots if I would work through the municipal hall's rezoning procedures to make it happen. I was game and began the nearly two-year process with Delta's Municipal Hall. By the time the prospect of bringing our rezoning to fruition was hopeful, some residents in our Kennedy Heights community had become concerned that excessively large homes were being built on small lots, which could devalue their existing properties. Negotiations with the Zoning Department delayed the subdivision process and tightened the building codes to ensure that future home construction would conform to newer regulations to control the house-size to lot-size ratio. Our subdivision request was approved pending no objections when neighbours were given the opportunity to appear at the public hearing. No one attended to object. After two years of my negotiating with Delta Municipal Hall personnel, our subdivision was approved with appropriate added restrictions. An interesting ancillary requirement was that upon completion of subdividing, two trees were to be replanted for each tree removed.

Position at Ohio State
Becomes Available

During the subdividing process, a friend who was a house builder offered to purchase the new vacant lot when it was officially registered with the New Westminster Land Titles Office. We listed our home for sale on October 17, 1992; it sold on November 2 with the buyer's caveat that we provide the official title documenting the legal dimensions of each lot. Both our newly subdivided properties had sold pending the registration with the Land Titles Office defining the now two separate properties. The moving van was scheduled for our move to Columbus, Ohio, on December 18, 1992.

There was another major event when I recognized divine intervention by giving me the position at Interwest Property Services for such a time as this. One week prior to our move from Canada to Doug's new position at The Ohio State University (OSU), our two properties were still titled as one. When we anxiously called Land Titles staff to check the status, we were told that there was a backlog on the registrar's desk. Just days earlier, due to our pending move, I had resigned from my Interwest position. Completely understanding the buyers' requirement that they have legal titling documents in hand before closing, I phoned Interwest's attorney. I shared my somewhat frantic concern with him. Within hours, the attorney called our home to advise us that the registrar's stack of pending titles on her desk had "gotten reshuffled." Our application had found its way to the top, and the registrations defining two properties were now complete and legally filed.

When we left Athens, Georgia, in 1971, Doug and I expected to live and work out his two-year contract in Canada. We moved back to the United States in 1992 after twenty-one years of life-changing career experiences and spiritual growth. While we were reluctantly leaving Canada, God was preparing us for our next incredible twenty-three years of living in the Columbus, Ohio, area. God has been so good. Doug and I have stood on the shoulders of giants who have been disguised as *just* ordinary folks.

Our decision to leave Canada was difficult. So difficult. We had planted ourselves so deeply that pulling up our roots was emotionally excruciating. Doug was gradually becoming discontent in his position as an associate professor at the University of British Columbia. He felt that he had been overlooked for some promotions that should have been his. After twenty-one years of teaching in UBC's Faculty of Education, publishing in professional journals, coauthoring a book, and presenting at a number of national and international conferences, he was never granted full professorship. Becoming discouraged and restless at work, Doug began to market himself.

In 1991, Doug applied for a position at The Ohio State University. He contacted Dr. Sigrid Wagner, a professor friend at the University of Georgia, to ask her for a letter of reference. Follow me in this sequence of events: Sigrid responded with regrets that she could not write the recommendation because she, herself, had applied for the same position. One year later, with Dr. Sigrid Wagner strategically placed in that coveted position at Ohio State, she notified Doug of another available position in the prestigious OSU College of Education.

At this juncture, both of us were experiencing some peace amid the bittersweet reality that we may indeed be leaving our beloved friends and our adopted country. Both our daughters were now married and living in Georgia. Grandchildren needed us to be nearer and dearer. My dad had died suddenly in 1985. Our remaining parents were aging. A dream position for Doug was a strong possibility. In February, I was sworn in as a Canadian giving me dual citizenship status to ensure that I would be documented for reentry whenever I wanted to or needed to return. Interwest Property Services partners closed the office so that my fifteen coworkers could witness my swearing-in ceremony.

Doug and I were at our fork in the road. I was in Atlanta with Sharilyn following the birth of our second grandchild, James Douglas, when Doug was invited to fly to Columbus to interview for the OSU position. In due time, he was called, offering him not only the position but the added status of tenured full professor. After weeks of struggling with the decision, Doug and I strolled around the peaceful lake in Burnaby Park on Victoria Day, May 18, 1992. We returned home, and Doug phoned to officially accepted Ohio State's offer. By this time, it was too late for the July 1 start date, so the offer was extended to become effective January 1, 1993.

Our grandbabies were popping in 1992. Elizabeth, our third grandchild, was born in late August in Columbus, Georgia. Doug encouraged me to book a stopover in Ohio on my return flight to Vancouver. I appreciated that Doug wanted me to have an orientation to the area before he officially resigned from his University of British Columbia position. I had been supportive throughout the Ohio State hiring process, but now that the first paragraph of our next chapter was imminent, Doug wanted me to continue to be involved and content with our shared decision.

Patti, one of Doug's future colleagues, met me at the Port Columbus International Airport, renamed John Glenn International Airport in 2016 to honor the memory of Ohio's native son, astronaut, and United States senator. Patti and I toured the Ohio State campus, attended a faculty barbecue, looked at available housing with a realtor, and I optimistically opened a bank account just in case we needed a bank with the capability to convert and deposit transferred Canadian dollars. Our friend, Sigrid Wagner, whom we had known from University of Georgia days, hosted me in her home and gave me the keys to her car for the weekend.

I had met Lane Avenue Baptist Church's music and youth director four years earlier when he was trumpeter at a wedding that Doug and I attended in Athens, Georgia. Having the keys to Sigrid's car, and with no other church connections in Columbus, it was an easy drive to the church building full of forever friends that I was about to meet for the first time. Two of those BFF were Dale and Rheva Blackwell, a couple the age of our parents. Dale, a successful college professor from Missouri, had tried unsuccessfully to retire from numerous jobs and was now enjoying a career as a realtor. I spent Sunday afternoon house shopping with Dale and being fascinated with the wit and wisdom of this elderly gentleman. In the days ahead, Dale kept in contact with Doug and me with home listings for our consideration based on our Sunday afternoon house-shopping experience. Doug and I flew to Columbus again in early December and, with Dale's help, left with a contract on a home that we would enjoy for the next twenty-three years.

With our move from Canada imminent, Sharilyn and seven-month-old James Douglas (JD) flew to Vancouver so that Sharilyn could see her friends and bid a final farewell to her childhood home place. By virtue of his mother's dual American and Canadian citizenship, James Douglas had the option to also become dual. Sharilyn, James Douglas, and I were the only ones present for the ceremony in the office with the citizenship judge. When the judge swore in the seven-month-old as a Canadian, he gently slapped him on the back and said, "Welcome to Canada. Go buy yourself a tuque and have a beer."

Doug had suddenly become anxious about the move to Ohio. Doug's uncertainty about whether we had made the right decision was bringing about signs of depression that took its toll on both of us. His dean at the University of British Columbia graciously granted Doug a three months' leave of absence. Knowing that he had a ninety-day option to return to his UBC position gave Doug some relief from the emotional pressures. Implementing the move was left to me to singlehandedly triage and pack up twenty-one years of belongings and memories. I was totally physically and emotionally drained.

It was moving day on December 18, 1992, and a rare heavy snowfall had slowed traffic to a crawl. As I wrote earlier, the Vancouver area was not equipped to handle the infrequent snow. The moving van's scheduled arrival was delayed and was finally loaded by late evening. Our contract with the moving company required that we be at the Ohio delivery destination on the designated date or pay $100 per day until the movers could unload our furniture at our new address. On December 19, exhausted and with a 2,500-mile drive, Doug and I stayed overnight in the Seattle area with close friends for the past twenty years, Jack and Mary Nell Roos. They have since retired and moved to Virginia. Ten years older than we, they remain among our dearest friends.

Other than skidding to avoid a stopped vehicle on the icy U.S. Route 2 through the crest of the Cascades at Stephens Pass, temporarily losing our cat, Shadow, in one of our motels and being unable to find an open restaurant or any place to buy food on Christmas Day, the trip otherwise went smoothly. With hunger pains and dressed in sweatshirts, jeans, and running shoes, Doug and I located and crashed an upscale Indiana hotel Christmas-dinner buffet event. Doug paid our bill as we entered the buffet lineup along with the other patrons who were dressed in suits, ties, and furs. Realizing that I was embarrassed because we were inappropriately dressed for the gala occasion, Doug reassured me by waving toward the endless buffet of elegance and whispering, "They don't know who we are, and they will never see us again. Bon appétit!"

Doug fastened a beautiful tennis bracelet on my arm when we arrived in Columbus, Ohio, on Christmas night 1992, and we stayed our first night in a motel. The treasured bracelet was my Christmas and welcome-to-our-new-home gift. Dr. Sigrid Wagner, our close friend from the University of Georgia days, who had alerted Doug about the OSU position that had ultimately brought about our move, was gracious to provide bed and breakfast for us during the following week until the closing on our Hillard home.

Remember the contract with the moving company that we signed in Canada to be available on a designated arrival date or pay $100 per day? It's too bad we failed to have the moving company reciprocally contract with us for a *per diem* if they failed to deliver our belongings on schedule. Days passed. We called the company regularly for a status report and were assigned and reassigned a "definite" date. Either Doug or I had to daily revise our schedule to ensure that someone would be at our empty home to receive our goods. Meanwhile, our local realtor and a handful of new friends had begun to lend us kitchenware, basic necessities, and a TV. As our patience wore thin near the end of two weeks of being held hostage by broken promises of delivery, we were informed that instead of the van's transporting our goods directly southeast to Ohio as promised, our goods had been offloaded into a warehouse in Edmonton, Alberta. How could a load destined for Ohio find its way off-route northeast to Edmonton? When a truck finally arrived, we learned from the movers, based in the Toronto area, that their company had been subcontracted to bring the trailer with our goods into the United States. The first attempt to deliver was turned back at the border because one of the original drivers had a criminal record. Our goods arrived the next day in surprisingly good condition, given the detours.

Before our December 1992 move to Ohio, our prior brief visits had impressed us that greater Columbus was an amicable metropolis of 1.2 million with a unique small-town milieu. We had lived in another country for twenty-one years and had comfortably adjusted to foreign cultural, political, medical, mortgage, tax, and investment regulations. We thought we were returning *home*, yet having lived away for so long, we had to relearn how to navigate unfamiliar day-by-day routines that once had been second nature.

Doug's Ohio State position began in early January, and I started the seemingly endless job of unpacking and transforming our house into our home. Neighbors welcomed us. We loved our house and community. Doug and I had soon planted ourselves deeply into the moderately conservative lifestyle of the Midwest. While I was finding myself busy, happy, and adjusting, within weeks, Doug became melancholy, irritable, and he could not sleep. I wondered if he had become disillusioned with his new dream job. He seemed to be fitting in well at OSU, church, and community, but he was different. *Different* to the extent that I stopped unpacking. The recurring thought haunted me, *Are we moving back to Vancouver?* Although I wanted to find a job and establish my identity in the community, I hesitated for fear it would be temporary. There were a few months of uncertainty, maybe close to a year before Doug got traction and soared!

Faye and Doug

By the time he retired nineteen years later, Doug was known throughout North America and beyond as a noted Ohio State researcher, contributor, and conference presenter for educating teachers about teaching and learning mathematics. Among numerous recognitions and awards, perhaps one of the most significant was a $3-plus million National Science Foundation research grant over five years that began in 2005.

Doug and I joined Lane Avenue Baptist Church where I had worshipped in August on my first visit to Columbus. We remained serving with that congregation and with the same pastor, Dr. Wayne Nicholson, for our twenty-three years in Ohio. As we always have, we poured ourselves into the church's ministries. Two of my most memorable volunteer responsibilities were chairing the stewardship committee and serving eleven years as director of the International Department, where a Bible study was available and free classes of beginning English were offered to accommodate several levels of learners. A hotel chain bought the church property in 2013 with its building in need of extensive and expensive upgrades. The sale of the church's real estate, which was ideally located in a commercial zone near the Ohio State campus, provided an opportunity for our congregation to relocate and rebuild in our Hilliard neighborhood. The church name was then changed to The Crossing Community Church.

We had moved from the Vancouver area in 1992, just as our church there was in planning stages to build an addition to the worship centre to accommodate an educational wing and day care centre. The following year, Sam and Marilyn Whitaker, friends in our new congregation at Lane Avenue Baptist Church, flew to Vancouver, where the four of us spent a week working alongside Royal Heights' members on the construction of their new building. Another Lane Avenue church couple generously donated their frequent flyer miles for Sam and Marilyn's flight.

Our new Columbus-area home was located at the entrance to a cul-de-sac, Shire Creek Court, with seventeen households. Passersby could not miss the SOLD banner sprawled across the realtor's sign, but they were unaware that their new neighbors had arrived two weeks earlier until the moving van eventually appeared in the street to unload. The next evening was cold and blustery with darkness falling early. The doorbell rang, and we were about to meet Bob, Hope, and fifteen-year-old Anna Taft. When they entered, the aroma of freshly baked bread followed them into the entrance hall. The five of us exchanged pleasantries as we sat among the clutter and unpacked boxes. Shortly, we were engaged in an introductory conversation. In response to Bob and Hope's inquiry about what had brought us to Columbus, we learned that Bob was Ohio's secretary of state and the great-grandson of President William Howard Taft. Anna, who was in the process of making friends with Shadow, offered to be our cat sitter. Upon our learning that Hope was a gardener, we were well on our way to bonding. Our friendship continued and strengthened throughout Bob's two four-year terms as Ohio's governor (1999–2007). Immediately following the inauguration of the new governor, Ted Strickland, in 2007, Bob and Hope left for a safari and much-needed respite. We were humbled to be the first friends they reached out to when they returned. Together, the four of us enjoyed a quiet dinner while looking through their album of safari pictures in a small but popular local Greek restaurant.

Hope's love for gardening served her and the state well in her role as Ohio's first lady. She brought to fruition her dream to bring native vegetation from the diverse regions of the state to beautify the Governor's Heritage Garden. Volunteers, all women until Doug retired and became the first male, gathered one day monthly to weed, plant, and maintain what became an alluring living legacy for the people of Ohio. One special occasion in the three-acre Governor's Heritage Garden was the ceremony to officially open a water garden, complete with a bridge and tiered fountain, that would be home to fish, turtles, and other Ohio water life. Dignitaries and media from throughout the state were in attendance, many bringing a container of naturally sourced water from his or her region. The samplings from Lake Erie, the Ohio River, Buckeye Lake, and other recognizable bodies of Ohio water were to be poured, respectively, into the water garden at a designated prompt. The ceremony was symbolic of consolidating the state's water systems into the one water garden. While Doug and I looked on, the announcer called the name of Shire Creek. Why, that's the small creek that our street is named for! At that moment, sweet Anna shoved into our hands a bottle of water that she had collected from Shire Creek. Like a parent nudges a reluctant preschooler, and with news cameras flashing, Anna gently pushed us to pour our water into the now-fused waters of the fountain to represent the creek that ran parallel to the court where we had shared many memories with the Taft family. It was a simple but special gesture affirming our friendship.

Once again, we reached out. Others reached in. Circles and bonds of friendship affirmed us. Before long, we were planted! We loved almost everything about Columbus: the small-town feel of America's fourteenth largest city with a population of slightly under one million, the convenience of navigating the city, the excellent medical care offered through Ohio State's integrated state-of-the-art medical system, and so much more. For the first time ever, we enjoyed having four distinct calendar seasons. Well, we enjoyed *three* of the four seasons. And for the first time since leaving Georgia in 1971, we had access to college football! To make up for our twenty-one-year deprivation, we applied for 1993 seasons tickets to the

Buckeyes home games. We had learned earlier that it could take a season or two to get through the lineup to qualify for purchasing the coveted tickets. We qualified for the tickets on our first try and were destined to be Ohio State Buckeye fans thereafter.

The Saturday after Thanksgiving has traditionally been the anticipated gameday for college football archrivals. In our Big Ten Conference, it is the Ohio State Buckeyes versus the University of Michigan Wolverines. To find and buy the coveted tickets has historically been stressful and expensive. My Robinson family reunion has been scheduled in south Alabama on that Saturday for decades, so our tickets for the game were always for sale. I arrived at my endodontist appointment a week before the big game, wearing my Buckeye shirt and earrings. In making conversation, my doctor asked if I was going to the game. I explained why Doug and I would not be going and, somewhat jokingly, asked if he would like to buy the tickets. He gave a negative response while he proceeded to inject the needle to numb my jaw for the root canal. He and I had earlier discussed that my dental insurance had been maxed out for the year, and I would owe $900 out of pocket for the procedure. The endodontist returned shortly to report to me that he had phoned his wife, and she wanted the tickets. He offered a deal: he would barter the root canal in exchange for the tickets. Everybody won, including the Buckeyes!

Our two daughters, sons-in-law, and four grandchildren gathered at our Ohio home annually around Independence Day. Debbie's family drove ten hours from Columbus, Georgia. Sharilyn's family had a more leisurely seven-hour drive from North Carolina. We scheduled numerous fun and memorable events around their visits.

David and Leah Canady were our next-door neighbors. Dave was the senior partner in a family-run trilateral business: tax preparation, investment management, and business management. It was in 1994 before I sensed that Doug had settled in, and I mentioned to Leah that I was ready to begin looking for a job. Upon learning from Leah that their Research Management office had an opening, I applied, interviewed, and was soon being trained by pregnant Melanie, who was planning to be a stay-at-home mom following the birth of her first child. I was given the assignment of manag-

162

ing investment client services plus ensuring that Securities Exchange Commission (SEC) compliance regulations were followed for the investment arm of the business that was affiliated with Raymond James and Associates Inc. The Research Management partners flew me to St. Petersburg, Florida, on two occasions for further training at the Raymond James headquarters campus. During the heavy workload brought by tax preparation during March and April, I helped with data input for clients' tax returns. Little did I realize that the exposure to tax preparation would be a skill I would utilize for years to come when I prepared our personal tax returns with the onerous challenge to correctly convert Canadian/U.S. currencies and tax-reporting slips to report our Canadian retirement income component. I retired from Research Management in May 2011 after working there for sixteen years. One caveat I requested when hired was that I would have the flexibility to travel on business trips with Doug when my work schedule allowed.

Travels in Southeast Asia, Europe, and Tennessee

And travel we did! I am appreciative for David and the other Research Management partners who allowed me to continue traveling the world with Doug as opportunities came. Doug's business-related travel expenses were covered by the institution or organization that invited him. Doug and I paid out of pocket for my transportation, meals, and any extra lodging cost for an additional person in the room. In 1989, while we were living in British Columbia, Doug had been selected by a Canadian government-funded UBC project for a four-week assignment with Regional Education Centre for Science and Mathematics (RECSAM) in Malaysia. I traveled to Southeast Asia with Doug following a week of Canadian government-sponsored intense orientation for both of us in Hull, Quebec. For four of the five weeks in Malaysia, we experienced the beautiful island of Penang. While Doug was involved as a consultant at RECSAM, I spent my days volunteering at the Malaysia Baptist Theological Seminary, cataloging on the computer all the resources available in their media centre. The Malaysian librarian of Chinese descent pressed me for more details when I told her that I had grown up in a small town in south Alabama. Wondering why she persisted, I finally responded, "Atmore." I was amazed when she told me that when she had been a student at Mobile College (now the University of Mobile), she regularly visited Atmore for ministry in the prison where my Pawpaw and Uncle Vernon had worked. It is indeed a small world! During our time there, Malaysia celebrated five statutory holidays allowing free time for us to enjoy short trips to Kuala Lumpur, Malacca, Ipoh, and Singapore. On the front end and back end of the Malaysian assignment, we experienced several fascinating days traveling in Macao, Hong Kong, and Bangkok.

When in Malaysia, 370 miles north of the equator, we welcomed the invitation of Doug's students to join them on the two- to three-hour hike through the jungle to the top of Penang Hill. There, we enjoyed the spectacular view and the welcomed relief of the less humid and more comfortable temperature of 70°–85°F, compared to the oppressive heat in the sprawling city of George Town below. The steep incline offered an optional funicular ride, but Doug and I chose the more adventurous and challenging experience. A couple of days after our hike accompanied by locals, Doug and I, now familiar with the route, packed our lunch of peanut butter sandwiches and plenty of bottled drinking water and began our leisurely trek through the humidity of the century-old virgin rainforest. Although the path was paved and not difficult, I chose a stick to assist when the trail was steep. Soon the melodious calls of the jungle birds were hushed when in our path ahead appeared daddy monkey, momma monkey, two adolescents, and a toddler. "Oh, how cute!" I exclaimed to Doug. To which daddy monkey showed his teeth and growled something in monkey language that I wasn't sure I understood, so he said it again, this time louder and with more teeth. Momma monkey must have liked what he communicated because she joined in and then was mimicked by the three young'uns. You know: monkey see, monkey do! With each snarl, the family closed in on us. I began to wave my stick swiftly to ward them off. Doug crouched behind me as closely as he could. Now realizing that I was the front line of defense, I swished the stick even more rapidly and wondered, *What's next?* At that moment, we heard the welcomed sound of an approaching motorbike. Until now, we had traveled the ascending trail totally alone. If this had been a movie, this was the cue for the William Tell Overture cadence. The rider was a Malaysian "Lone Ranger," appearing not on a horse named Silver but on his Honda. He sensed our danger risk more than we did. The cyclist scrambled from his seat, grabbed a handful of rocks, and began to throw them, striking the metal guardrail with loud pings. The monkey family, processing that reinforcements had arrived, gave one last sinister growl and retreated into the jungle. Our hero said they wanted our lunch. Doug acknowledged that he knew they wanted the food. I was annoyed that Doug didn't just give the beasts the lunch and save us from that frightening encounter. Doug didn't want to eat the food from the outdoor vendors at the top of the hill.

Although we were living in Columbus, Ohio, in 1994, the University of British Columbia reached out to Doug with a repeat similar RECSAM contract to revisit Penang, Malaysia. We piggy-backed trips on the front and back ends of this travel opportunity to visit friends in Singapore and Thailand. Again, I volunteered at the Malaysia Baptist Theological Seminary, working this time in the seminary president's office to key in a revised handbook for the students.

While in Malaysia, with the assistance and advice from RECSAM business office personnel and their Thai connections, we arranged and purchased a tour of Thailand. Each day for several days prior to the Thai tour, Doug and I went to the ATM that had a relationship with our U.S. bank. One stood to guard while the other withdrew the maximum M$400/day until we had withdrawn enough to pay for the tour in advance. On our own, we enjoyed a short stay on the beautiful Thai resort island of Phuket in the Andaman Sea. On the next leg of the tour, we flew to Chiang Mai, where we shopped at the famous Night Market. We were surprised that the arranged "tour" we met the next morning consisted of a van with a Thai-speaking driver and an English-speaking Thai guide. It was not a coach filled with tourists as we had expected—just the four of us. A day later, at the conclusion of a river cruise with our guide and a boatman, the van driver retrieved us to continue.

At the end of our five-day impressive tour, our Buddhist guide expressed an interest in our being Christians. This gave me an opportunity to tell her about my relationship with Jesus. She told me that she had a friend who had a Bible, but she did not have one. While she and the driver waited, I ran into our hotel room, got the Gideon Bible that I had observed the night before was written in both English and Thai. Our guide was excited to have a Bible that she could read with her Christian friend. When I reported to the clerk at our hotel's front desk that I had given away the Bible that was in our room, she responded that they had a box full and would replace it. Doug and I have always supported The Gideons International organization, but even more so after that meaningful opportunity to be able to place a Bible in the hands of someone who, hopefully with the encouragement of her Christian friend, has been introduced to Jesus.

On yet another Southeast Asia assignment in September 1996, Doug taught for four weeks at a teachers' college in Malang, Indonesia. On one weekend, we flew to the resort island of Bali. Southeast Asians are notorious for their gracious hospitality and having *people connections* to meet whatever need or request they perceive a guest may have. A Bali police officer met our flight at Bali Airport Denpasar. Either the officer or his *people* checked regularly on our welfare during the weekend to ensure our safety and enjoyment. When we returned to our Malang hotel, we were bothered that, without our permission, all our personal belongings left in our hotel room had been removed and stored elsewhere in the facility while the room that we were paying for had been rented to other guests during our absence.

A top attraction, while based in Malang, behooved us to depart our hotel at midnight for a three-hour ride with four of Doug's Indonesian students to the active Mt. Bromo volcano, 7,641 feet above sea level. Our agenda was to be on the rim of the volcano for the five o'clock sunrise. After walking about an hour across the "sand sea" (desert floor), we climbed three hundred-plus steps to the rim. It was pitch dark except for the stars of the Southern Hemisphere, which seemed to dangle almost within reach. The sunrise was breathtaking. It was at daybreak when we realized that we were sharing the narrow rim of the caldera with an estimated three hundred others. The warmth from the molten lava radiated from the crater on our left. On our right, a sheer cliff dropped more than 7,600 feet to the sand sea below. There were no barriers nor park rangers to ensure anyone's safety. All spectators had ascended and descended the mountain at their own risk to view the spectacular sunrise. The temperature at dawn was around 40 degrees Fahrenheit.

We traveled to Europe in September 1997 and enjoyed the first leg of our trip lodging and touring with Jannie and Roel, Dutch friends living in Enschede, the Netherlands. We next traveled by train to Brussels and Bruges, Belgium, then via ferry and train, arriving in London four days following the funeral of Princess Diana. The vast spread of memorials, both in height and breadth, throughout the city was overwhelming and left an enduring image. That scene, accompanied by the somber mood of the thousands who had gathered to grieve at both Buckingham and Kensington Palaces, is a poignant memory.

Princess Diana's Memorial Flowers

Security on horseback was everywhere until I needed it. Unable to locate an officer, I approached a woman who had pilfered through the accumulated memorabilia of flowers, teddy bears, and trinkets that had been left in memory of the beloved princess. The marauder had found a replica of Diana's tiara, and I watched her stuff it underneath her jacket. Even though the thief apparently did not speak English, she understood my body language that doggedly would not let her walk away with the symbol of nobility. Doug sat quietly, finishing his lunch on a bench nearby while watching me unrelentingly insist that she put it back. He knew that in the end, the plunderer would not win! She gave up and, at least while we were present, returned the tiara.

Doug and I traveled to many North American educational conference venues where Doug was often invited to attend as a presenter. One of the most remarkable for me was held in Nashville in March 2003. My plan was to hop on a trolley tour bus and spend my first day exploring the historic city. Dressed appropriately in jeans, an Ohio State sweatshirt, and walking shoes, my first stop after leaving our hotel room was at the concierge desk. The attendant excitedly informed me of the call she had just received from the Ryman Auditorium ticket office. Just half an hour before Eddy Arnold was to donate much of his country-music memorabilia to the Country Music Hall of Fame, a group of tourists had canceled. They were holders of four of only 250 coveted tickets to the prestigious ceremony. Sadly (for them), they had contracted a foodborne illness making their seats available. The concierge asked if I would like to attend. If yes, I would need to claim a free ticket within fifteen minutes, adding that the Ryman was a ten-minute walk. As I rushed out the door, the concierge called to put a hold on a ticket in my name that would be held for me at will call. She didn't mention the dress code!

Approaching the Ryman, and out of breath, I saw long lines of fans and dignitaries gathering for the ceremony. One more observation: they were dressed in suits, ties, dresses, and high-heel shoes! Look at me. Somewhat embarrassed, but not enough to miss this opportunity, I confidently approached the will call window to receive my admission to the ceremony. I waited in line behind and talked to Robert Macon, grandson of Uncle Dave Macon, who was one of the original three to start the Grand Ole Opry. Soon enthralled by the two-hour ceremony, highlighting some of Eddy's many top hits, I forgot about my apparel and was captivated by every moment. I could imagine hearing Doug's typical prompt in similar circumstances, "Just enjoy this. They will never see us [you] again." Brenda Lee, Jack Clements, Suzy Boggas, Glen Rieff, Bobby Bare, Billy Burnett, Jim Lauderdale, and others shared memories and songs.

To close the event, Jack Clements led the audience in singing "And When I Dream" with Eddy sobbing in the background. So far, so good!

After the ceremony, I was walking through the grand corridor of the Ryman toward an exit. I turned in response to a tap on my shoulder and looked into the face of none other than Eddy Arnold. I could not believe my ears when he asked me to join him, his wife Sally, family, and the other dignitaries for lunch that was set up in an adjacent room! I graciously declined, and this time, my attire was the reason. He engaged me in a conversation about the Ohio State Buckeyes football team. I have often wondered why he invited me to join that celebratory lunch. Was it because he liked Ohio State, or did he think I was homeless? Sally, Eddy's wife of sixty-six years, died in March of 2008. Eddy's death followed two months after Sally's.

Family Gatherings:
Providential Watchcare

It was comforting to be closer to immediate family for times of celebration and grieving during the years ahead. We were nearer, at least stateside, when my dear father-in-law's health began to fail. We were glad that Doug's parents had flown to Columbus in 1995 to see our home. They, being farmers, were interested in and shared advice about our backyard garden. The four of us enjoyed the Columbus Zoo and other outdoor venues to escape the monotonous news of the O. J. Simpson trial. Four years later, we knew that the end of Theodore's earthly life was near. The first time that Doug traveled alone to check on his dad, he decided to get a roundtrip flight from Columbus to Pensacola. When Doug arrived at the hospital, he called to report that his father was not likely to live much longer. I scrambled to get our house, lawn, pet, car, and clothing organized for an emergency thirteen-hour trip. I did not sleep one wink the night before driving, alone, the 800 miles. Rather than tossing and turning, I considered just getting into the packed car and driving. Then the "what-if" thoughts entered my mind: In the darkness, I may have an unlikely car malfunction or an accident, or I will need to have a rest stop. I would not feel safe going alone into a rest area during the wee hours. At 5:00 a.m., I arose from my sleeplessness and began my journey empowered by the prayers of family and friends and the loan of my neighbor's cell phone. On my last house walk-through before leaving, I checked my wallet for coins in case I needed to call from a pay phone. Having none,

I scooped up the only three quarters I could find laying on Doug's chest of drawers.

That trip was the most reassuring awareness of God's presence that I have experienced. As I was driving alone through the dense fog about an hour into my eight-hundred-mile trip and halfway between Columbus and Cincinnati, suddenly, three deer stood facing me in the middle of Interstate 71. I gently braked, not knowing which direction to steer nor how the three would react. Each deer, one behind the other, gracefully and fearlessly walked close to my car and stood peacefully peering through the window at me before continuing their saunter to the shoulder of the road. Several hours later, my sleepy eyes were almost impossible to keep open. With 300 miles remaining to my destination, I pulled into Alabama's Welcome Center to get some much-needed caffeine. I was proud of myself for collecting the three quarters from Doug's chest of drawers for the coin-operated beverage dispenser. Not a problem, I thought, when I discovered that the coke vending machine now required four quarters, and I had only three. I can get a bill changed into coins in the Welcome Center gift shop. There was a huge sign on the gift shop door that read, "Sorry. We cannot make change." Physically and emotionally exhausted, I opened my purse to put the bill back into my wallet. The zipper on my coin purse was open, exposing four quarters! Hours earlier, I had put three quarters into my empty change pouch. I dropped four quarters into the coin slot and consumed my miraculous caffeinated coke. Dazed by this experience, but refreshed, I continued south on Interstate 65. Approaching Georgiana, Alabama, I knew that I was unlikely able to safely continue one more hour to my destination without a nap. For the first time ever, when I was the driver, I felt myself nodding. Immediately, there was a flutter in my face. Startled, I snapped out of my dozing to brush away the "butterfly" that apparently had gotten into my car at Alabama's Welcome Center. There was no visible living creature in the car with me. But I knew I was not alone. I safely, and now wide awake, continued my drive to the home of my parents-in-law. I shall never forget. I was *not* alone!

Doug's widowed mom continued to live at the farm homeplace. The remaining two-acre homestead that included the house would, at Verta's demise, pass to Doug's only sibling Roger who had farmed for twenty years in partnership with his father, Theodore. Doug had signed a legal document years earlier agreeing that his parents' property should be passed to his brother and sister-in-law. Roger and Sandra had always lived in Atmore and had been the go-to advocates when any help was needed as Theodore and Verta aged. Before Theodore and Verta sold their farmland and their expensive equipment was auctioned at a significant loss during the farming recession of the 1980s, Roger had shared the responsibility of planting and harvesting the crops. Yes, the remnant of those glory days rightly belonged to Roger and Sandra, who had invested their lives in the land.

In the fall of 2002, Verta was diagnosed with colon cancer. After surgery, her surgeon recommended a dual regimen of chemotherapy followed by radiation. The family cringed at the thought of this aggressive treatment for our eighty-three-year-old matriarch. It was no surprise that this iron lady had determined to conquer the malignant beast that had taken up residence in her abdomen. With grit and determination, she began treatments in Brewton, Escambia County's government seat, thirty miles away. My stepmom, Beryl, regularly drove Verta for her chemo treatments. The family was encouraged that she maintained the strength to function on her own. Verta was radiant when she reached her ambitious goal to attend the New Year's Eve wedding of her only grandson, Terry, and his bride, Valerie.

During the 2003 school spring break in March, and with Verta's permission, Doug and I contacted all available in the Owens family to gather for a reunion at Verta's house. Still living on her own with little assistance, she agreed that I could organize a potluck and roast a hen for the main course. She was chipper that day, wearing her fanny pack that contained a small pump to send chemo medication into her resolute body through a port near her collarbone. She enjoyed her day of pruning and dragging limbs along with the rest of the family as we all joined in to assist with various chores.

A month later, when radiation had been added to the regimen, Verta's frail body began to decline rapidly but would then rally somewhat. On Easter Sunday morning, Doug and I received the dreaded yet expected call from Roger that her homegoing was imminent. Having already packed our luggage in anticipation of this news, we loaded the only roadworthy car of our two and turned the key to start. The battery was completely dead. All car repair stations routinely open on Sundays were closed for Easter. Finally, the AAA service truck arrived. The mechanic's only option was to charge the dead battery because he did not have a replacement. His advice was to not shut the engine off until we got a new battery installed. With thirteen hours of hard driving ahead, we made it an hour south on I-71 to an open-for-business truck stop and repair garage for 18-wheelers. Upon hearing our story of trying to get to our dying relative's bedside, an auto mechanic was called to help. The mechanic, not affiliated with the truck-stop business, phoned his son, who was manager of the local auto parts store and interrupted the family's Easter dinner gathering. Although the parts store was closed for Easter, the store manager left his family dinner, opened his shop, brought and installed the appropriate battery. Learning of our travel route into Cincinnati, he motioned toward the ominous low-hanging clouds and warned us that serious weather was approaching. Physically and emotionally drained, we pushed on through the severe storms. When we arrived in Birmingham, three hours from Atmore, we learned that Verta had passed.

Another round of emotionally draining news came in 2005 when Sharilyn's seventeen-year marriage ended. What we had feared for several years surrounding their rocky relationship was now a reality. Accompanying the news of an impending divorce came Sharilyn's disclosure to us that during her marital struggles, she had become addicted to alcohol and was presently in a recovery program. At this writing, Sharilyn has now been sober for over sixteen years, faithfully participating in her program and mentoring other women who are engaged in the hard work of recovery. Sharilyn's marriage to Randy on January 1, 2010, brought new hope as our close-knit family gathered with Randy's family to celebrate. Sharilyn's husband, Randy, is an educator in addition to being an outstanding bluegrass musician. In 2019, Cisco Networking Academy recognized Randy for his being in the top 25 percent globally for positive student feedback and performance.

Restoration, Reunions, Recreation

Doug, along with colleagues, applied for and received a noteworthy $3-plus million National Science Foundation research grant over five years beginning in 2005. Those five years consumed and energized Doug, who assumed the role of principal investigator for the Classroom Connectivity in Promoting Mathematics and Science Achievement (CCMS). He traveled extensively throughout the United States and into Canada to observe classrooms whose teachers were participants in the study. Sharilyn, a math educator, joined the team, assisting her dad in observing North Carolina, South Carolina, and Massachusetts teachers in classrooms using Texas Instruments technology. In 2008, Debra and I joined Sharilyn in Massachusetts. During the days when Sharilyn was busy with her CCMS responsibilities, Deb and I explored Plymouth Rock's rich history. Sharilyn joined us in the evenings for meaningful girl time when the three of us met for evening dinners and tours.

All nine of our immediate family met in Vancouver for the fortieth anniversary of Royal Heights Baptist Church. In preparation for the 2007 trip, Doug and I were elated when we reviewed our Delta Skymiles statements and discovered that between the two of us, we had enough frequent-flyer miles to underwrite roundtrip flights for our seven accompanying family travelers. The bad news was that my share of redeemable miles was subject to immediate expiration due to inactivity. Solution: Without delay, generate some activity such as subscribe to yet another magazine to secure the miles. With assured success, Doug and I proceeded to step two, and we reminded each traveler that valid passports were required, effective January 23, 2007, to enter and depart Canadian airports. This was a requirement of the Western Hemisphere Travel Initiative enhanced security requirements following the September 11, 2001, terrorist attack. All except Debbie had been issued passports previously. When getting information together for Debra's application, Greg discovered that his government-employee passport, with a shorter validity span than regular, had expired. The invalid passport stories ceased to be humorous when a couple of weeks before departure, Sharilyn retrieved James Douglas's and Emily's passports from the security of their safe box. Both of the children's passports had expired. Similar to Greg's government-issued passport, James Douglas's and Emily's passports were issued as minors' passports with a shorter valid period. What had appeared to be one passport lacking for Debra evolved into four passports needed on short notice. With assistance from their U.S. senators and congressional representatives, all passports arrived in the nick of time, flights were booked with our frequent flyer miles, and the Vancouver trip was a successful, memorable experience for our grandchildren to visit their moms' childhood homeland. We once again acknowledged that we were under the guarded watch of angels.

So our calendar flipped to 2011. Doug and I remembered well our first travel adventure with People-to-People International Ambassadors Program when we experienced a magnificent tour of China in 1999. With memories of climbing the steepest path to the top of the Great Wall, visiting the phenomenal excavation site of the terra cotta warriors in Xi'an and much more, we were enthusiastic to again travel with People-to-People when two opportunities became available in 2011. During June, we served as delegates with People-to-People's Peace Initiative to Turkey. Our tour administrator and guide was Mary Jean Eisenhower, granddaughter of President Dwight David "Ike" Eisenhower. The objective of People-to-People was and is to develop a grassroots relationship among people internationally. I was fourteen years old in 1956 when President Eisenhower founded the program and encouraged high school students to become pen pals with foreign teenagers. For many years, I exchanged letters, ideas, and gifts of friendship with an Italian teenage boy, Gianfranco, and a British teenage girl, Valerie.

The second extraordinary adventure with People-to-People International as our trip organizer was the rare opportunity to tour Cuba. Our group was among few Americans who had been allowed to visit the island since 1963 when, during the Cuban Missile Crisis, President John F. Kennedy prohibited all travel for U.S. citizens to Cuba. Our People-to-People tour group was allowed by the United States government to enter the otherwise forbidden country under an educational/cultural special permit license from the Office of Foreign Assets Control. We were advised to never dispose of those official documents that permitted us to enter the socialist country ruled by the authority of Marxism.

The Cuban trip was dubbed educational. It was without a doubt *educational* for our travel group. To start, upon our arrival at the Havana Airport, Doug snapped a picture of the shrink-wrapped luggage coming down the chute for pickup on the baggage carousel. We were intrigued that bags were shrink-wrapped, obviously to prevent pilfering. Immediately, airport security demanded that Doug delete the picture. He complied.

There are two official Cuban currencies: Peso Cubano (CUP) and the Cuban dollar, also known as the peso convertible (CUC). The convertible peso is used on the international market and is the one most commonly given to tourists as exchange. The CUP is worth about 1/24th of the CUC, and it is the everyday medium of exchange used by Cubans. Cuba is perhaps the only country with the rare frustration of negotiating two currencies.

The island was beautiful and the people, poor. Once imposing buildings were crumbling and in dire need of repair. The restoration of some buildings had been undertaken by large European corporations. The iconic classic American cars of the 1950s were seen everywhere, a memorable step back in time. Our American tour leader alerted us that all our scheduled events had been preapproved by Cuban authorities, but agendas were subject to cancellation on short notice. Indeed, our visit to a cosmetology school that trained single moms was canceled with no explanation the day we were scheduled to visit the facility.

Another tense situation occurred when the driver of our large made-in-China tour bus had to make several attempts to navigate a hairpin curve on a country road. Shortly after the maneuver, our bus was pulled over by authorities. We, the passengers, were anxious when our driver was called from the bus to discuss the incident. A Texan, who was one of our delegates, discreetly translated for us the conversation taking place in Spanish outside the bus. Apparently, the officers were suspicious that the backup cameras were espionage cameras that activated when our bus driver backed up several times to negotiate the tight bend. The authorities were eventually convinced that we tourists were not using any surveillance equipment or spying. We did get the message that our every move was being monitored.

We were told by our local guide at the time of our 2011 visit that pork, chicken, lamb, rabbit, and fish were common menu entrées for the locals. Beef was in short supply and expensive, but it was usually on the tourists' menus in restaurants and on hotel buffets. Sadly, beef was not available to locals other than to Cuban children, pregnant women, or those on medical diets, although restaurant and resort employees were permitted to serve the entrée to tourists. We were told that the government kept a strict inventory of livestock. If a cattleman lost a head of cattle to death, a government official was notified to view the carcass to document that the animals had indeed died and that it had not been butchered for personal consumption. Laws were enforced to combat the flourishing black market. Breeders were fined if their cow(s) had strayed. Prison sentences of up to three years were handed down for unauthorized persons owning a cow. Three months to a year imprisonment was likely for processors who purchased the meat of illegal cattle and four- to ten-year imprisonment possible for cattle theft and slaughter.

Cubans were restricted from accessing other than state-authorized media. In order to prevent exposure to world news, hotel housekeeping staff was not allowed to watch cable television while servicing guest rooms. They lived in a bubble, seeing and hearing only what their government allowed and having only pirated exposure to the rest of the world.

When our educational/cultural tour came to an end, we shared among ourselves the incredible Cuban experiences and the striking contrast to our own freedoms, too often taken for granted. We stood in line at the airport security check with our passports in hand. Our tour leader, Troy, left the group to dutifully get our collective tickets to Miami. After a period of waiting, we realized how long that we had stood in line, and we began to discreetly express our anxiety, one to the other. Troy soon appeared and, with trepidation, quickly gathered our travel documents from us. Sensing Troy's anxiety, some were reluctant to relinquish their valued passports. At Troy's insistence, he took all passports into a side room for what seemed to be too long. When he reappeared, he quickly returned our respective passports and urged each of us to head for the plane that had been delayed for our immediate boarding and departure. Our group of about forty was instructed to leave the airport, ask no questions, go straight to the tarmac, board the plane, sit in any available seat, and hold our luggage on our laps. After our safe arrival in Miami a short time later, Troy told us that our original departing flight had been canceled. With permission from People-to-People International, Troy had paid Havana airport authorities $12,000 ($300 US per 40 passengers) so that we could leave in time to catch connecting flights in Miami to our respective destinations.

Retirement: Juggling Parental Care with Personal Care

I retired in May 2011 after sixteen years of employment with Research Management Inc. Doug retired one month later, with the distinction of professor emeritus, from The Ohio State University. Timed in almost perfect sync with our retirements came Mother's fall and subsequent pelvic injury in Mobile. A couple of years earlier, with her permission, I had taken over Mother's accounting to ensure that her bills were paid accurately and on time. In the process, I had met Mother's insurance agents, bankers, and other local administrators of her business interests and had given them my contact information. A few months later, Mother's insurance agent phoned to alert me that Mother had been at fault in about six somewhat minor auto accidents in as many months, causing her monthly auto-insurance premiums to soar in excess of $600. The agent strongly suggested that it was time for me to consider taking her car keys. I had accompanied Mother to her neurologist a few weeks earlier, who had given the same advice. This was a difficult but inevitable judgment call for Mother's protection, as well as for the safety of others.

Mother's brother, my Uncle Levi, who lived in the greater Mobile area, was my rock and support through all the ensuing decisions that lay ahead. This included removing her car to his place. Doug and I had prearranged with Mother's church friends for her transportation so that Mother could be with her close friends in her Bible study group and in worship service. Intensifying our concern for Mother's safety, we learned from her friends that she had not only refused to use her walker but also her cane. We hired Mother's neighbor, Annie, who earned her living as a caregiver, to check on Mother twice daily, help with grocery shopping, count and administer medication, and help with and alert us of any additional needs.

When we returned to Mobile from Columbus, Ohio, a month later, Uncle Levi had found a buyer for Mother's car. The transfer of title in exchange for cash payment had been scheduled to coincide with our visit. The night before the transaction, I gently broke the news of the car sale to Mother. Unsure of how she would react, I asked her if she would like to meet the buyer and sign the transfer documents. She said she would think about it. I had power of attorney to act on her behalf if needed, but I did not play that card. The next morning, Mother was in her best dress, well groomed, and chatting with her friends on the phone. I overheard her say that she had sold her car and was on her way to the bank to complete the sale. I somewhat felt a reprieve that Mother had been allowed to maintain her dignity among her peers. I liked that.

For eighteen years, Mother was settled in and felt secure in the familiarity of her two-story apartment in the Spring Hill community of Mobile. She enjoyed visiting her friends who were quite content and adjusting well in assisted-living facilities, but Mother was adamant that she was not going to move. Her church friends checked on her regularly and had begun to phone or write to alert me of their observations of Mother's mental and physical decline. After a few sessions of prescribed home care therapy, Mother refused to let the therapists into her apartment. As evidence of her inability to safely live alone progressed, our thirteen-hour drives from Ohio to south Alabama became more frequent with extended stays.

At this time, my stepmother's ongoing physical health issues were beginning to manifest. Until then, Beryl had managed to care for herself independently, with family and friends regularly visiting or phoning to check. For four years following our retirement, Doug and I monthly drove the thirteen-hour trip to south Alabama and remained for a week to care for my two moms. Their personalities were quite contrasting. Mother was demanding, bitter, and uncooperative compared to Beryl's sweet, gentle spirit of "not wanting to be any trouble" for her family. Mother's onset of dementia was somewhat responsible for her contrary behavior. Admittedly, she was never an easy person to get along with. I attribute her distrust and suspicions to pent-up bitterness from her early adulthood when she lost two hard-fought custody battle attempts to keep her only child.

Beryl passed at age eighty-four in March of 2014. I was privileged to give my sweet stepmom's eulogy. Mother's death followed on December 19, one week before her ninety-fourth birthday.

On the Road Again

By the time we celebrated our fiftieth wedding anniversary in 2012, Doug and I had experienced international travel to nineteen countries and had lived in Canada with landed-immigrant status for twenty-one years. Since that milestone anniversary, we have added ten more international tours to our travel repertoire. Doug and I are awed, and we bow amazed when we recount these adventures. On countless occasions when we have found ourselves in an exotic place, we humbly recall our modest beginnings. We never dreamed when we excitedly crossed the mighty Mississippi River for the first time with our three-month-old baby to visit Mother and Johnny in Shreveport that many more doors of adventure and opportunity were yet to come. *Carpe diem*!

Sharilyn introduced an idea in 2013 that Doug and I join her and Randy for a road trip. She had shared stories of her childhood in Canada with Randy, her husband of three years. Randy's fascination was so stirred about his wife's hometown that he, a gifted musician, wrote a song (my favorite) entitled "Vancouver." As if we needed further incentive, both Sharilyn and Randy had friends, originally from North Carolina, offering accommodations at their home in Anchorage. This fantasy soon advanced to and through the planning stages to reality. Doug and I left Columbus, Ohio, in our 2000 Toyota van boasting 150,000 miles and drove to Vancouver, stopping for bed and breakfast along the way with strategically placed friends. Sharilyn and Randy, not retired as Doug and I were, flew to Vancouver to begin their two weeks' vacation. We stayed a few days to show off Vancouver and to validate Randy's musical tribute to the city. Then we skirted civilization for a couple of weeks as we drove north to Alaska into Yukon Territory through Watson Lake, Whitehorse, and Dawson. We eventually drove the impressive final lap on the Top of the World Highway into Chicken, Alaska. Legend has it that the town was to be named for the ptarmigan, a game bird in the grouse family that abounds in the area. None of the residents knew how to spell ptarmigan, so they settled on the catchy name, Chicken.

The four of us hired a private fishing guide and boat for a day on the Kenai River at a total cost of $1,000. Together, we caught three fish. We were at least consoled that we had not purchased insulated shipping crates while shopping the night before when we were more optimistic about our anticipated fishing excursion. When we arrived at our fishing spot on the river, our guide fully suited us with appropriate gear and necessities for fishing and surviving in the secluded wilderness, including toilet tissue and a can of bear spray.

After Doug and I began our trek back to Ohio, Randy and Sharilyn enjoyed a helicopter tour and walked on glaciers in Denali National Park. When Doug and I arrived home, again having stopped with friends along the route, our trip odometer had clocked 11,570 miles. Our only minor delay was to have a flat tire repaired. Thankfully, we were only 20 miles from civilization in Tok, Alaska, after having traveled hundred-mile remote stretches seeing only bears, elk, bison, and other beasts of the wilderness.

In the summer of 2018, Doug and I, along with our daughter, Debra, ambitiously drove the roundtrip from Athens, Georgia, to Vancouver, Canada, and beyond, covering 7,400 miles in three weeks. Debra's husband, Greg, had planned to accompany us, but knee issues prevented his sitting for a long trip. On March 30, Debra tumbled from her hammock and broke her arm, requiring a plate and nine screws. Debra was on board by June's travel date. She didn't miss a beat, including hiking through nine national parks, Graceland, Great Salt Lake, and Mt. Rushmore, meanwhile doing her share of driving. Sharilyn flew to Vancouver to join us for a weekend of celebrations and reunions. Doug and I, together with our adult daughters, walked down memory lane to personally revisit people and places and to relive the events that had, in so many ways, significantly defined each of us.

A highlight of our Canadian trip was a reunion arranged predominately through social media with many of our Royal Heights Baptist Church friends. Just before the Royal Heights building was sold, I contacted as many friends and members as I could. The people I reached relayed the message to their network and so on. As a result of our viral outreach, eighty former members gathered at the building on July 7, 2018, each with a bag lunch to reminisce through memories and music and to encourage a remnant of the remaining fragile congregation. Their last pastor had convinced some members and others to put their credence and investments into his apparent Ponzi-like scheme resulting in those individuals' losing their savings. According to the February 19, 2019, issue of the *Surrey Now-Leader* local newspaper, former Royal Heights pastor "Alan Braun, his son Jerry Braun, and White Rock's Steven Maxwell (also known as Steven Fassman) were found to have taken $450,000 from two investors in three separate transactions." Thousands, who were impacted by Royal Heights' fifty-one years of outreach and ministry, continue to grieve the closure of that once dynamic, now scattered, church and its mission.

Relocating to Athens and Reconnecting to Family

Sound counsel from retiring Ohio church friends, who were moving to be near family in Texas, continued to resonate. Doug, as well as I, replayed their comments about their relocating while they were physically and mentally able to connect to new friends, church, and community. Paul and Bonnie advised that if aging parents wait until their family is compelled to uproot them from their comfort zones, the transition is tough on everyone. With that shared wisdom, Doug and I discussed the eventual need to relocate, sooner rather than later.

We had long considered the rolling foothills of north Georgia's Blue Ridge Mountains as our potential retirement destination. Years earlier, we had quickly assimilated into Athens community life during our three years when Doug was a doctoral student at the University of Georgia. When we lived in Canada and Doug was granted two years (1980–81 and 1987–88) respective study leaves, we chose to return to Athens.

Our grandson, JD, currently serves as associate pastor to children and congregational life at a church in Macon, Georgia. In 2015, when he was a divinity-school student serving part-time on staff at Commerce (Georgia) First Baptist Church, he alerted us that he would be preaching in his senior pastor's absence on Memorial Day weekend. We had already made plans to attend my extended Robinson family reunion in Alabama in early June. Doug and I decided that we could detour through Georgia, hear JD's message, and then look around Athens a bit to investigate potential neighborhoods, availability, and housing costs. Except for renting temporary accommodations during the two year-long sabbaticals, we had not lived in that area for forty-four years.

Our son-in-law, Greg, now living in Columbus, Georgia, had grown up in Athens, the "Classic City." He recommended a realtor to show us homes that might be suitable based on our list of prerequisites sent to her earlier. If the property did not have an established vegetable garden, it must have an ideal location to cultivate one. On Memorial Day, the realtor showed us perhaps half a dozen homes. Nearing the end of time that she had allotted for us, we asked to look again at a previously shown home that had potential. Both Doug and I independently knew that this was the house. The dilemma was that our intention was to simply get a feel for neighborhoods and costs, but we were not considering a move for perhaps another couple of years. Our Ohio home needed to be updated to get it ready to market.

The following Sunday morning, while en route back to Ohio, we made an offer. The offer was accepted. We hesitantly asked if the closing could be delayed for three months until August 31, buying some time for us to ready our Ohio home for listing, find a realtor, and, hopefully, find a buyer. We doubted that the late August closing would be acceptable to the seller. We were once again stunned. The renters of the Athens home had a special-needs teenager. They were renting our newly contracted home until *September 1,* when their home under construction would be ready for occupancy! The renters had feared that we, the buyers, would want to move in right away, thus disrupting their teenager's rigid schedule. Our suggested closing date was perfect for everyone. Following our closing in Athens at the end of August, we owned two homes for seven months. Having two homes, one in Ohio and one in Georgia, when November's falling temperatures warned that Ohio's winter was imminent, we hired a van to move our belongings to Georgia's more moderate climate. The sale of our Ohio home closed in March 2016.

We treasure the enriching experiences and enduring friendships bestowed upon us when Atmore, Troy, Montezuma, Athens, Vancouver, and Columbus were *home* to us. The opportunities and memories are countless, and almost every acquaintance impacted our lives in a constructive way. We seamlessly transitioned back to our Southern roots after having lived in Canada for twenty-one years and in Ohio for twenty-three years. Only God knew that on the near horizon, we would need to be near to provide consolation for and to receive encouragement from our immediate and extended families.

Much joy and many festivities surrounded our oldest grandchild, Thomas's, June 2016 marriage to his sister Elizabeth's childhood friend, Emily.

Family Picture

Our families and Emily's families were forever bonded in the celebration of their union. Thomas was aware that his Emily was bipolar, but with their commitment and her medication, they vowed together "until death do us part." Sadly, that tragic day was six months into their marriage when Thomas arrived home from work to find that his beloved wife had taken her life. Emily was a princess bride buried in her wedding dress. The hundreds of mourners who attended Emily's funeral service were urged to seek professional help for themselves or loved ones who were exhibiting any warning signs indicative of possible bipolar or other mental disorders.

Following Emily's death, our grandson, Thomas, moved from Albany, Georgia, to a new job in Charlotte, North Carolina, where he eventually met and fell in love with Nicole. There was a twinkle in his eyes, and joy had returned to his broken heart. Family and friends gathered to celebrate the March 14, 2020, marriage of Thomas and Nicole, one day before the national COVID-pandemic lockdown.

Doug and I had planned to continue to Ohio from Thomas and Nicole's wedding in Charlotte. I was prepared with tax slips and documents to get our 2019 state and federal tax returns ready for filing by using the tax program available to me every year, courtesy of my former employer since my 2011 retirement. Soon after leaving the wedding celebration, a vehicle moved into our lane, causing significant damage to the front driver's side of our 2019 Ford Edge. The other driver was cited with illegal lane change, and the investigating officer gave a cautious okay for Doug and me to drive the crippled Edge for another hour to Sharilyn and Randy's home. That accident, serious enough to cause significant body damage to our car but not inflicting injury to any of the four people involved, was providential in our decision two days later to abandon the Ohio travel plans and return home to get our car into a body shop. Meanwhile, resulting from the escalating spread of COVID-19, Ohio's Governor DeWine moved quickly to put his state on lockdown. If we had traveled to Columbus, we likely could not have returned home until weeks later.

While adding finishing edits to this manuscript, our hearts again break for Thomas. Ten months into their marriage, Nicole left to visit her family in Boston. She returned to the apartment where she and Thomas lived to collect her belongings and move back with her family. The emotional pain may cause one to feel that the broken heart can never heal. Then I reread pages of my story. I am reminded throughout of God's providence, presence, and faithfulness. Regardless of what happens to us or to those whom we love, the heart of God never stops protecting, loving, and reaching.

In September 2016, food and laughter surrounded us in Athens where we, along with Renato's and Elizabeth's families and friends, celebrated Renato's surprise proposal to our granddaughter, Elizabeth. All of us had kept the proposal a secret for just about as long as we could. Renato is an art instructor of Brazilian descent who taught at the same Clarke County (Georgia) elementary school as Elizabeth. They were married in May 2017 with a befitting tribute to deceased Emily, Elizabeth's friend and sister-in-law, who was to have been one of Elizabeth's bridesmaids. Renato and Elizabeth live near us in Athens, Georgia. Renato is employed as department head for visual arts at a local arts school. Elizabeth and Renato will give us our first great grandchild, Oliver (Ollie), early in 2022.

Referencing the tender emotional bond that I shared with my paternal grandparents, particularly with Mammaw, someone asked how I would like for my grandchildren to remember me. I hope that he/she/they could say, "Grandmother loved me. She and Granddaddy 'O' were always available to give their support. Whether we were on their laps, in their arms, or on their shoulders, we were always in their hearts and always in their prayers. Grandmother and Granddaddy 'O' were *just* folks." My story began with *just* folks whose affirmation never gave me cause to doubt who I was nor Whose I am. I have two grandchildren in the LGBTQ+ community. While I don't understand it, I love them dearly. I know that the same God who has guided me over the mountains and through the valleys of my life also holds them in His own loving hands.

Passing the Torch

I have documented numerous occasions when family, friends, and strangers looked beyond themselves to cheer me on as a little girl, as a teenager, as a young and middle-aged adult, and now as an elderly woman. They were and are *just* folks, ordinary people, who have graciously and often sacrificially offered a hand, a smile, words of encouragement or advice, a shoulder, or a listening ear. My hope is that future generations will continue to sow and reap that trait of altruism.

Through the amazing technology of matching and tracking one's genetics through deoxyribonucleic acid (DNA) to a common source, I have recently been introduced to many of my ancestral icons and their stories passed posthumously. Now in the winter season of my life, I am indebted to ancestors who bequeathed a priceless legacy: not bank accounts, not investments, not jewelry nor property, but the inherent gifts of faith, values, integrity, a work ethic, and perseverance.

One's family legacy is a fragile gift preserved to pass to posterity. I think of the one passing the legacy as having a greater impact than one who has the esteemed privilege to carry the Olympic torch. The general public can nominate everyday heroes from their communities to potentially become an Olympic torchbearer. The selection process for the torch relay is filtered through the scrutiny of the organizing committee and the sponsoring companies. Often, torchbearers are *just* folks who have overcome personal challenges or who have inspired others to remain strong in the face of adversity. Just as my ancestors have passed their heritage from their generations to mine, the eternal Olympic flame symbolizes the continuity between the ancient and the modern: the past, the present, and the future. There are backup sources to relight in the event a torch begins to flicker or die out during the endurance of the relay. At last, the highly guarded secret identity of the final torchbearer, traditionally a hero athlete of the host country, is revealed and has the honor of lighting the Olympic cauldron. All the fires from the first flicker of the initial flame in Olympia, Greece, to the final moment several months later trace back to a common source. I have endeavored in my story to convey the perseverance and grit of those who came before me by passing their legacies to their, and now to my, descendants. One's heritage has been entrusted to the next generation at great cost.

Contrary to Mother's excited proclamation at my birth, I seriously doubt that my dimples were planted by an angel's kiss. However, I am keenly aware of countless divine interventions. I cannot know how many times God's protective hand has safeguarded me, but I do know that I have felt the brush of angels' wings. "For he will command his angels concerning you to guard you in all your ways; they will lift you up in their hands so that you will not strike your foot against a stone" (Psalm 91:11–12 NIV).

Writing this story has been my aspiration for several years. I kneel amazed when I think of what might have been, but God has been faithful with His strategic placement of circumstances and *just* folks. When transposing my memories into a manuscript, my initial purpose was to leave these memoirs as a legacy for my family and close friends. During the writing process, many have encouraged me to disseminate the story more broadly. My hope is that as you have read my story, you have also recalled *just* folks who have at some time lifted you onto their shoulders. I pray that you will also be inspired to encourage some struggling family members, friends, or strangers. Then may you, my dear readers and *just* folks, also bow amazed.

Praise for *On the Shoulders of Just Folks*

You never know the details of your neighbor's life-defining experiences. That was true in my case when Faye Robinson Owens asked me to read her book, *On the Shoulders of Just Folks*. I knew from conversations we had shared over neighborhood dinners that Faye had many special people in her life, but I did not realize how the positive impact of *just* folks had prepared her for life's challenges until I turned through the pages of her childhood. Her experiences reinforced for me resiliency research that stresses the importance of *just* folks in the lives of every youth. A trusted adult's positive influence during one's formative years can be the encouragement she or he may need to navigate later obscure situations. It's a great read that takes you from Faye's angel-kissed dimples as a baby through her many life transitions in various parts of the world and to her eventual return to her Southern roots. Along the way, it is evident that faith, family, and friends worked together to positively impact her life—and she challenges her readers to fill that role for others.

Hope Taft
Friend, neighbor, and first lady of Ohio (1999–2007)

There is something endearing and compelling in the honest recounting of a life well lived. With candor and clarity, Faye Robinson Owens allows us to sojourn with her through every decade of her life. She does not shy away from those profoundly difficult life experiences that have punctuated her life since birth. However, her highs and lows provide a rich and textured tapestry on which the faithful providence and provisions of God are put on display. We need more autobiographies like this. There is a simplicity in Faye's storytelling, and the cumulative effect of the stories she tells is a personal compulsion to recognize the gracious hand of God in our lives and how often He has captured our imaginations and caught us up into the grand movement of His working in our world.

Rob Blackaby, PhD
President
Canadian Baptist Theological Seminary and College
200 Seminary View • Cochrane • AB • T4C 2G1 • Canada

Nothing is as encouraging as a fresh, well-told story about the highs and lows of life. Faye Robinson Owens in *On the Shoulders of Just Folks* writes with the charm of a southern lady, the honesty of a counselor, and the transparency of a friend. It blessed me, and I know it will bless you.

Phil Waldrep
Phil Waldrep Ministries
Decatur, Alabama

About the Author

Faye learned at an early age that God has a plan and purpose for each of us, but she was middle-aged when she looked through her life's rearview mirror and realized the timely and strategic placement of people and circumstances along her life's path.

Faye saw her dad for the first time, the day before her third birthday, when he arrived home from WWII combat. After learning of his wife's infidelity, divorce proceedings ensued. Only nine months after meeting his child, Faye's father was awarded custody by a judge who was apparently sympathetic toward a returning soldier whose wife had been unfaithful during his three and a half years of military deployment. But God had already implemented His plan for Faye's care and destiny.

She grew up in the home of her loving paternal grandparents, married her high school sweetheart, raised two successful daughters, traveled in thirty countries, and lived twenty-one years in another country where God continued to provide opportunities for her spiritual growth. Over the years, Faye's family and friends have listened with interest. Inspired by her story, they have encouraged her to chronicle her life's journey. She has accomplished that feat. Now with her amazing story published, readers can affirm God's faithfulness throughout the challenges of her life's journey—and theirs.

CPSIA information can be obtained
at www.ICGtesting.com
Printed in the USA
LVHW030423270722
724446LV00001B/113